THE BIRDWATCHER'S THREE-YEAR RECORD BOOK

NOTES & ILLUSTRATIONS BY

JOHN HILLS

SWAN·HILL
PRESS

First published in the UK in 1998
by Swan Hill Press, an imprint of Airlife Publishing Ltd

British Library Cataloguing-in-Publication Data
A catalogue record for this book
is available from the British Library

ISBN 1 85310 963 0

Typeset by Servis Filmsetting Ltd.
Printed in Hong Kong

Swan Hill Press
an imprint of Airlife Publishing Ltd
101 Longden Road, Shrewsbury, SY3 9EB, England

INTRODUCTION

We all know when the swallows return and we know that it is at more or less the same date every year, but are we as certain about the day they leave? Do they spend the same amount of time with us each year? Just how much effect does each summer's weather have on the number of youngsters they successfully rear? This book is intended to help you record information and provide you with some answers.

At the beginning of every month you will find a checklist of bird species: three boxes have been provided alongside the name of each bird, one box per year. By simply ticking off the species you have seen each month, you will be creating a personal record of your sightings. The remainder of the month has daily entry spaces and can be used in much the same way as a conventional diary. By cross-referencing year to year, week by week you will be able to monitor changes in bird behaviour. Highlighting for example the effects of climatic changes, building developments or changes in farming practices on the birds in your locality.

There are numerous excellent books on birds and bird behaviour, which collectively provide a wealth of knowledge. Your own notes I am sure will prove that there is still a lot to learn. They can also help when it comes to being certain about what we think we have seen. We all have a reluctance to think we have spotted something out of the ordinary. A few years ago I was convinced that I had seen a white stork flying up the valley where I live. I made a note of the date and the locality and a few days later rang an area bird recorder. He was able to confirm my sighting, as other birdwatchers had reported seeing the same bird in the area on approximately the same date. Over the years, your entries will build into an informative record of all aspects of your birdwatching activities, and no doubt provide a few surprises too.

JANUARY CHECKLIST

YEAR	1	2	3
DIVERS			
Red-throated diver			
Black-throated diver			
Great Northern diver			
GREBES			
Little grebe			
Great crested grebe			
Red-necked grebe			
Slavonian grebe			
Black-necked grebe			
SHEARWATERS			
Fulmar			
Cory's shearwater			
Great shearwater			
Sooty shearwater			
Manx shearwater			
Mediterranean shearwater			
STORM PETRELS			
Storm petrel			
Leach's petrel			
GANNETS			
Gannet			
CORMORANTS			
Cormorant			
Shag			
HERONS			
Bittern			
Night heron			
Little egret			
Great white egret			
Grey heron			
Purple heron			
IBISES			
Spoonbill			
DUCKS			
Mute swan			
Bewick's swan			
Whooper swan			
Bean goose			
Pink-footed goose			
White-fronted goose			
Greylag goose			
Snow goose			
Canada goose			
Barnacle goose			
Brent goose			
Egyptian goose			
Shelduck			
Mandarin			
Wigeon			
American wigeon			
Gadwall			
Teal			
Mallard			
Pintail			
Garganey			
Shoveler			
Red-crested pochard			

YEAR	1	2	3
DUCKS (cont.)			
Pochard			
Ring-necked duck			
Ferruginous duck			
Tufted duck			
Scaup			
Eider			
King eider			
Long-tailed duck			
Common scoter			
Surf scoter			
Velvet scoter			
Goldeneye			
Smew			
Red-breasted merganser			
Goosander			
Ruddy duck			
HAWKS			
Honey buzzard			
Black kite			
Red kite			
White-tailed eagle			
Marsh harrier			
Hen harrier			
Montagu's harrier			
Goshawk			
Sparrowhawk			
Buzzard			
Rough-legged buzzard			
Golden eagle			
OSPREYS			
Osprey			
FALCONS			
Kestrel			
Red-footed falcon			
Merlin			
Hobby			
Peregrine			
GROUSE			
Red grouse			
Ptarmigan			
Black grouse			
Capercaillie			
PHEASANTS			
Red-legged partridge			
Grey partridge			
Quail			
Pheasant			
Golden pheasant			
Lady Amherst's pheasant			
RAILS			
Water rail			
Spotted crake			
Corncrake			
Moorhen			
Coot			
CRANES			
Crane			

YEAR	1	2	3
OYSTERCATCHERS			
Oystercatcher			
AVOCETS			
Black-winged stilt			
Avocet			
THICK-KNEES			
Stone curlew			
PLOVERS			
Little ringed plover			
Ringed plover			
Kentish plover			
Dotterel			
Golden plover			
Grey plover			
Lapwing			
Turnstone			
SANDPIPERS			
Knot			
Sanderling			
Little stint			
Temminck's stint			
White-rumped sandpiper			
Pectoral sandpiper			
Curlew sandpiper			
Purple sandpiper			
Dunlin			
Buff-breasted sandpiper			
Ruff			
Jack snipe			
Snipe			
Woodcock			
Black-tailed godwit			
Bar-tailed godwit			
Whimbrel			
Curlew			
Spotted redshank			
Redshank			
Marsh sandpiper			
Greenshank			
Green sandpiper			
Wood sandpiper			
Common sandpiper			
PHALAROPES			
Red-necked phalarope			
Grey phalarope			
SKUAS			
Pomarine skua			
Arctic skua			
Long-tailed skua			
Great skua			
GULLS			
Mediterranean gull			
Little gull			
Sabine's gull			
Black-headed gull			
Ring-billed gull			
Common gull			
Lesser black-backed gull			

YEAR	1	2	3
GULLS (cont.)			
Herring gull			
Iceland gull			
Glaucous gull			
Great black-backed gull			
Kittiwake			
Sandwich tern			
Roseate tern			
Common tern			
Arctic tern			
Little tern			
Black tern			
White-winged black tern			
AUKS			
Guillemot			
Razorbill			
Black guillemot			
Little auk			
Puffin			
PIGEONS			
Rock dove			
Stock dove			
Wood-pigeon	✓		✓
Collared dove	✓	✓	✓
Turtle dove			
PARROTS			
Ring-necked parakeet			
CUCKOOS			
Cuckoo			
BARN OWLS			
Barn owl			
OWLS			
Snowy owl			
Little owl			
Tawny owl			
Long-eared owl			
Short-eared owl			
NIGHTJARS			
Nightjar			
SWIFTS			
Swift			
Alpine swift			
KINGFISHERS			
Kingfisher			
BEE-EATERS			
Bee-eater			
HOOPOES			
Hoopoe			
WOODPECKERS			
Wryneck			
Green woodpecker			
Great spotted woodpecker			
Lesser spotted woodpecker			
LARKS			
Short-toed lark			
Woodlark			
Skylark			
Shore lark			

YEAR	1	2	3
SWALLOWS			
Sand martin			
Swallow			
House martin			
PIPITS			
Richard's pipit			
Tawny pipit			
Tree pipit			
Meadow pipit			
Red-throated pipit			
Rock pipit			
Water pipit			
Yellow wagtail			
Grey wagtail			
Pied wagtail			
WAXWINGS			
Waxwing			
DIPPERS			
Dipper			
WRENS			
Wren	✓	✓	
ACCENTORS			
Dunnock	✓	✓	✓
THRUSHES			
Robin	✓	✓	✓
Nightingale			
Bluethroat			
Black redstart			
Redstart			
Whinchat			
Stonechat			
Wheatear			
Ring ouzel			
Blackbird	✓	✓	✓
Fieldfare			
Song thrush			
Redwing	✓	✓	
Mistle thrush	✓		
FLYCATCHERS			
Cetti's warbler			
Grasshopper warbler			
Savi's warbler			
Aquatic warbler			
Sedge warbler			
Marsh warbler			
Reed warbler			
Icterine warbler			
Melodious warbler			
Dartford warbler			
Subalpine warbler			
Barred warbler			
Lesser whitethroat			
Whitethroat			
Garden warbler			
Blackcap		✓	
Pallas's warbler			
Yellow-browed warbler			
Wood warbler			

YEAR	1	2	3
FLYCATCHERS (*cont.*)			
Chiffchaff			
Willow warbler			
Goldcrest			✓
Firecrest			
Spotted flycatcher			
Red-breasted flycatcher			
Pied flycatcher			
REEDLINGS			
Bearded tit			
TITMICE			
Long-tailed tit			
Marsh tit			
Willow tit			
Crested tit			
Coal tit	✓	✓	✓
Blue tit	✓	✓	✓
Great tit	✓	✓	✓
NUTHATCHES			
Nuthatch			
CREEPERS			
Treecreeper			
ORIOLES			
Golden oriole			
SHRIKES			
Red-backed shrike			
Great Grey shrike			
Woodchat shrike			
CROWS			
Jay			✓
Magpie	✓	✓	✓
Chough			
Jackdaw			
Rook		✓	
Carrion crow	✓	✓	✓
Raven			
STARLINGS			
Starling	✓	✓	✓
SPARROWS			
House sparrow			✓
Tree sparrow			
BUNTINGS			
Lapland bunting			
Snow bunting			
Yellowhammer			
Cirl bunting			
Ortolan bunting			
Little bunting			
Reed bunting			
Corn bunting			
FINCHES			
Chaffinch	✓	✓	✓
Brambling		✓	
Serin			
Greenfinch	✓	✓	✓
Goldfinch		✓	✓
Siskin		✓	✓
Linnet			

YEAR	1	2	3
FINCHES (*cont.*)			
Twite			
Redpoll			
Arctic redpoll			
Crossbill			
Scottish crossbill			
Scarlet rosefinch			
Bullfinch			✓
Hawfinch			

NON-LISTED SIGHTINGS

The great spotted woodpecker is a bird of woodlands, parks and large gardens. It frequently visits bird-tables when its natural food becomes scarce in the winter months.

JANUARY

YEAR 1 2002. MAX 6.5°C MIN −7°C **1st**	MAX 6°C MIN −6.5°C **2nd**	MAX 6.5°C MIN −6.5°C **3rd**	MAX 4.5°C MIN −3.5°C **4th**
~~Blackbird~~ 3	Robin Coal tit	Blackbird 4	Bluetit
~~Bluetit~~ 2	Blackbird ♂&♀ Chaffinch (M)	Mistle Thrush.	Blackbird 2
~~Dunnock~~	Bluetit	Collared dove 2	Great tit
~~Great tit~~	Mistle Thrush	Magpie	Dunnock
Robin	Collared dove 2		Mistle thrush
Chaffinch	Great tit		Robin
	Greenfinch		Coal tit
	Dunnock.		Collared dove 2

YEAR 2 CURRENT 6°C MAX 8.5°C MIN 2°C **1st**	CURRENT 5.5°C MAX 7.5°C MIN 0°C **2nd**	CURRENT 1°C MAX 2.5°C MIN −2.5°C **3rd**	CURRENT −2°C MAX 2.5°C MIN −3.5°C **4th**
Collared dove 2	Starling 3 Dunnock 2	Blackbird 2 Dunnock 2	Blackbird 2
Coal tit	Greenfinch ♂3	Starling 2 Crow	~~Bluetit 2~~
Great tit 2	Blackbird	Bluetit 2	Chaffinch 2
Chaffinch (F)(F) 2	Bluetit 2	Greenfinch ♂4	Greenfinch 5
Starling 3	Magpie	Chaffinch (F)(M) ♂4	Collared dove 2
Blackbird	Chaffinch (F)(M)(F) 2	Collared dove	Dunnock 2
Greenfinch 6	Collared dove 2	Wren	Starling 5
Bluetit 2	Blackbird	Robin	~~Siskin~~
Robin		SNOW	

YEAR 3 SNOW! 3" **1st**	Showery, warm. **2nd**	Snow, sprinkling on top of... **3rd**	Sun lvl 2 **4th**
Blackbird 2 Starling 3	Greenfinch 14	Blackbird 2 Collared dove	Jay
Chaffinch 3 Great tit	Starling 3 Great tit	Starling 2 Coal tit	Dunnock 2
Greenfinch ♂5	Bluetit 2 H.Sparrow	Greenfinch ♂4	Chaffinch 2
Dunnock	Chaffinch 2	Chaffinch 2	Greenfinch 4
Collared dove ♂7	Dunnock	H Sparrow	Collared dove
Bluetit 2	Jay	Dunnock	Blackbird
H. Sparrow	Collared dove 4	Robin	
Goldfinch 5	Blackbird	Jay	
Goldcrest	Coal tit	Bluetit 2	

JANUARY

ADDITIONAL NOTES:
* First siting this winter
2004 1st. ⚥ Goldfinch! 1 Goldcrest

FOG 5th	FOG SUN. WK2 6th	7th
MAX 11°C MIN 1·5°C	MAX 6·0°C MIN 2°C	MAX 10·5°C MIN 5°C
Bluetit ♂3	Great tit — Chaffinch (F)	Wren
Great tit	Bluetit 2 — Collared dove	
Robin	Robin — Wren	
Blackbird 2	Redwing *	
Dunnock.	Mistle thrush	
	coal tit	
	dunnock.	
	Blackbird 2	
		Leeds

CURRENT −0·5°C	CURRENT 0°C (10am) 6th	CURRENT −3°C 7th
SUN WK2 5th		
MAX 4°C MIN −2·5°C	MAX 0°C MIN −3·5°C	MAX 2°C MIN −4°C
Dunnock 2 — Brambling 3*	Collared dove ♂4 — Dunnock 2	Brambling (MF) 24
Blackbird 2 — Chaffinch	Bluetit 2 — Starling 2	Great tit — Goldfinch 2*
Bluetit 2 — ~~Starling~~ *	Greenfinch 2	Bluetit — Chaffinch 2
Coal tit	Blackbird	Greenfinch 4 — Collared dove 2
Starling 2	Chaffinch 2	Dunnock — Wren
Robin	Robin	Blackbird
Collared dove 2	Brambling 3*	Starling 2
Greenfinch	Great tit	Robin

Warm & damp 5th	Overcast, rained in night 6th	Cloudy 7th
Chaffinch 2	Blackbird	Blackbird
Bluetit	Greenfinch	Bluetit 2
Greenfinch 2	Collared dove ♂3	Chaffinch 3
Collared dove 3	Dunnock 2	Dunnock 2
	Jay	Greenfinch 2
		Robin
		Collared dove 3

The impressive great grey shrike is an uncommon but regular winter visitor. It favours the eastern side of the country and often returns to the same location year after year.

Great grey shrike

JANUARY

_{9am}

Year 1

8th — MAX 10°C MIN. 2.5°C	9th — FOG ALL DAY MAX 7.5°C MIN 2.5°C	10th — CURRENT 1°C MAX 7.5°C MIN 0.5°C	11th — CURRENT 6°C MAX 10°C MIN 0.5°C
Blackbird 3	Bluetit 2	Collared dove 2	Bluetit 2
Bluetit 2	Blackbird 2	Blackbird	Blackbird 2
	Dunnock	Bluetit 2	Mistle Thrush
	Magpie	Great tit	Starling 3
	Collared dove 2	Dunnock	Magpie 2
		Chaffinch	Robin
			Dunnock

Year 2

8th — CURRENT 1°C MAX 4°C MIN -2.5°C	9th — CURRENT 1.5°C MAX 5.5°C MIN 1°C	10th — CURRENT 1.5°C MAX 5°C MIN -0.5°C	11th — CURRENT 2.5°C MAX 9°C MIN -1.5°C
Blackbird 2	Bluetit 2	Bluetit	Blackbird 2
Bluetit 2	Chaffinch	Chaffinch 2	Bluetit 2
Brambling 3	Greenfinch	Greenfinch 2	Robin
Greenfinch 2	Blackbird 2	Dunnock	Greenfinch 4-8
	Starling 2	Blackbird	Starling 2
	Collared dove 2	Collared dove 3	Chaffinch 2
	Dunnock		Dunnock 2
	Robin		

Year 3

8th — Rain, heavy at times	9th — Overcast, cold wind	10th — Overcast. F. mild	11th — Sun- to/c 3. Sunny breezy wind & rain showers later
Bluetit	Blackbird	Blackbird 2 Siskin 3	Blackbird Robin
Dunnock 2	Robin	Starling 4	Bluetit Coal tit
H. Sparrow 2	Chaffinch	H. Sparrow 3	Collared dove 2
Greenfinch 6	Dunnock 2	Dunnock 2	Greenfinch 2 3 4 5 6
Chaffinch 2		Greenfinch 3	Chaffinch 2 3
Great tit		Collared dove 2	Goldfinch 2
Collared dove		Crow	Dunnock
		Bluetit	Bullfinch 2
		Chaffinch 2	H. Sparrow

JANUARY

CURRENT 9°0 12th
MAX 11°C   MIN 0.5°C

Helmsley

SUN. WK 3. CURRENT 7°C 13th
MAX 14°C MIN 6.5°C
Bluetit 2
Dunnock
Blackbird 23
Robin
Collared dove
Greenfinch 35

9am Current 7°C 14th
MAX 12°C MIN 3°C
Bluetit 2
Dunnock
Blackbird
Magpie

ADDITIONAL NOTES:
* First time this Siskins winter 2003 2004. Siskins 10th Bullfinch (pr) 11th

CURRENT 2°C 12th
SUN WK 3
MAX 10°C Min 2°C
Starlings 8   Bullfinch 2 (MF)
Bluetit 2   Robin
Blackbird 2   Siskin *
Greenfinch 25 Goldfinch
Dunnock
Redwing *
Chaffinch 2
Coal tit
Collared dove

CURRENT 9.5°C 13th
MAX 11°C   MIN 8°C
Greenfinch 4
Dunnock
Collared dove 2
Robin
Chaff

WINDY

CURRENT 10°C 14th
MAX 10.5°C MIN .6.5°C
Robin
Chaffinch (MF) 23
Greenfinch 45
Wren
Bluetit 3
Starling 4
Collared dove 2

WINDY

Cloudy, odd shower 12th

Blackbird
Siskin 2
Bullfinch (F)
Greenfinch 2
Chaffinch 23
Bluetit
Collared dove 4
Starling 2
Jay 2

13th
Collared dove 24
Greenfinch 36 H. Sparrow
Coal tit   Siskin
Dunnock 2   Starling
Blackbird
Chaffinch 23
Goldfinch
Crow
Bluetit

14th
Starling 4   Siskin 9
Blackbird 2   Bullfinch (M) (F)
Jay 2
Chaffinch 2
Collared dove 234
Dunnock
Bluetit 2
H. Sparrow
(Hospital)

At a glance, these two species of winter-visiting swans can be difficult to tell apart. The illustration shows adult and juvenile examples of both whoopers and Bewick's. Whoopers (top) have longer necks and larger yellow patches on their bills, giving them a distinctive elongated head shape.

Whooper and Bewick's swans

JANUARY

YEAR 1 9am Current. 3°C 15th	9am Current 6°C 16th	9am Current. 10°C 17th	Current 9am 3°C 18th
MAX .12°C MIN 3°C	MAX 12°C MIN 3°C	MAX 12°C MIN 1.5°C	MAX 10°C MIN 2.5°C
Bluetit 2	Dunnock	Dunnock	Blackbird 2
Robin	Robin	Blackbird	Bluetit 2
Blackbird	Blackbird 2	Bluetit 2	Dunnock 2
	Bluetit	Collared dove	Crow

YEAR 2 CURRENT 6°C 15th	CURRENT 7.5°C 16th	CURRENT 10°C (10.15 am) 17th	CURRENT 4°C 18th
MAX 10°C MIN 5°C	MAX 11.5°C MIN 6°C	MAX 10°C MIN 2.5°C	MAX 11°C MIN 3°C
Greenfinch 12	Chaffinch (M)(F)	Blackbird 2	Starling 6 Collared dove
Blackbird	Blackbird 2	Greenfinch 24	Great tit 2 Wren
Bluetit 3	Bluetit 2	Starling 12!	Chaffinch 2 Bullfinch (M)(F)
Siskin	Greenfinch 3 4 5	Collared dove 4	Bluetit 2 3 Brambling (F)
Collared dove 5	Collared dove 3	Brambling 2	Greenfinch 6
Chaffinch 2		Chaffinch	Robin
Starling		Bluetit	Blackbird
		Crow 2	Dunnock 2
			H. Sparrow

YEAR 3 Steel - rain pm. 15th	Dull, windy. 16th	Fine, sunny later frost overnight last night 17th	10k 4 Sun Hard overnight frost. Fine! 18th
Blackbird	Blackbird 2 Bluetit	Bluetit 2 H. Sparrow	Bluetit 2 Rook
Bluetit 2	H. Sparrow 2	Blackbird Collared dove 2	Collared dove 2 Robin
Collared dove 2	Greenfinch 8	Greenfinch 2	Blackbird 2
Chaffinch 2	Chaffinch	Chaffinch 2 3	Dunnock
Dunnock 2	Dunnock	Dunnock 2	Chaffinch 2
	Collared dove	Bullfinch 2	Starling 2
	Bullfinch 2	Goldfinch 2	Greenfinch 3
	Goldfinch	Siskin 4	H. Sparrow 2
	Siskin	Starling 3	Siskin

JANUARY

Current 9.40 6°C **19th**	Sun. Wk 11 Current 10am 10°C **20th**	Current 8.35am. 13°C **21st**
MAX 11°C MIN 5°C	MAX 14°C MIN 7°C	MAX 13.5°C MIN 6.5°C
Bluetit	Blackbird 2	Collared dove
Robin	Robin	Bluetit
Great tit 2	Mistle thrush	
Crow	Collared dove	
Blackbird	Bluetit	
Mistle thrush		
Collared dove 2		
Dunnock		

CURRENT 6°C SUN WILL **19th**	CURRENT 7°C **20th**	CURRENT 6°C **21st**
MAX 8°C MIN 2°C	MAX 11°C MIN 2.5°C	MAX 8.5°C MIN 3.5°C
Bluetit 24 Great tit 2	Greenfinch 4	Blackbird 2
Blackbird 23 Long tailed tit 2	Starling ♀ 12	Starling 259
Starling 6♀11 Wren	Bluetit	Chaffinch 2 (F)
Greenfinch 4 Robin	Chaffinch	Greenfinch 57
Chaffinch 3 (2FM) Coal tit	Great tit	Dunnock 2
Great tit 2 Collared dove 2	Robin	Bluetit 2
Bullfinch 2 (MF)	Blackbird 2	Collared dove 23
Dunnock	Collared dove 2	Great tit 2
	Dunnock	

V. Windy, dark clouds **19th**	Raining **20th**	Cloudy, but fine **21st**
Greenfinch 47 Starling 9	Starling 2 Great tit	Blackbird 2
Chaffinch 2	Collared dove 2	Woodpigeon 2
Bluetit 2	Bluetit	Greenfinch 6
Collared dove 5	Blackbird 2	Chaffinch
Siskin ♂ 4	Greenfinch	Bluetit 2
Jay	Chaffinch 2	Siskin 2
Blackbird	Siskin 56	Goldfinch
Dunnock	Goldfinch	Dunnock 2
Goldfinch	Dunnock	

ADDITIONAL NOTES:

Arriving each winter in varying numbers, bramblings often join flocks of resident chaffinches. Both species feed on seeds. When these mixed finch flocks are disturbed and take flight, the white rump of the brambling distinguishes it from its relatives.

Brambling

JANUARY

YEAR 1

22nd — Current 8.15am 7°C, MAX 10°C MIN 5°C	23rd — Current Temp 8.45 8.5°C, MAX 12°C MIN 5°C	24th — Current temps 9am 5°C, MAX 7°C MIN −1°C	25th — Current temp 1.5°C (9am), MAX 12.5°C MIN 1.5°C
Blackbird	Blackbird	Blackbird	Great tit
Bluetit 2		Tits —	Bluetit 2
Mistle thrush			Woodpigeon
Dunnock.			Blackbird 2
			Robin
			Mistle Thrush.
			(Snow around 10 cm. Did not lie)

YEAR 2

22nd — Current 5°C, MAX 9.5°C MIN 4°C	23rd — Current 4.5°C, MAX 11°C MIN 4.5°C	24th — Current 8.5°C 10.65°C, MAX 11°C MIN 7°C 7.5°C	25th — Current 7.5°C, MAX 10°C MIN 5°C
Bluetit 2	Greenfinch 3	Greenfinch ♀♂5	Bluetit 2
Greenfinch ♂4	Bluetit	Chaffinch (F) 2 Great tit	Collared dove 2
Robin	Collared dove	Collared dove 2 Blackbird	Blackbird
Chaffinch (m)	Starling 2	Bluetit 2	Chaffinch (F) 2
Goldfinch 2		Dunnock	Starling 4
Starling 3		Starling	Greenfinch ♀♂4
Dunnock		Wren	Great tit
Collared dove		Siskin 3	Coal tit
	Out most of day.	Robin	Bullfinch (F)

YEAR 3

22nd — Mild, cloudy some showers	23rd — Mild, cloudy	24th — Colder fine sunny	25th — SUN WK 5 (GBW Count)
Blackbird 3 Jay	Dunnock 2	Collared dove	Sparrow 4 Goldfinch
Starling 2 Collared dove 2	Blackbird	Chaffinch ♂3	Greenfinch ♀8 Jay 2
Chaffinch 2 Dunnock 2	Chaffinch 2	Blackbird 2	Bluetit ♀3 Coal tit
Greenfinch ♀♂8 Magpie 2	Goldfinch 2	Greenfinch 2	Blackbird 2 Siskin
Siskin 2	Siskin	Starling	Starling ♀3 Robin
Goldfinch ♀♂4	Greenfinch 3	Bluetit	Chaffinch 2 Crow
Robin		Dunnock	Collared dove ♀4
Bluetit 2		Siskin Squirrel	Great tit 2
H. Sparrow 2			Dunnock 2

26th
Current 9am. 10°C
MAX 11°C MIN 6.5°C
- Blackbird 2
- Dunnock
- Bluetit 2
- Robin
- Collared Dove 2
- Greenfinch 3

27th
Sun wks. Current 10.45 8.5°C
MAX 13°C MIN 5°C
- Blackbird 4
- Collared dove
- Bluetit
- Robin
- Dunnock

28th
Current 9am. 6.5°C
MAX 10.5°C MIN 6.5°C
- Blackbird

These familiar little acrobats can struggle to survive spells of intensely cold weather when food becomes hard to find. A regular supply of peanuts will provide a lifeline for the birds and an excellent opportunity for us to observe their antics at close range.

26th
CURRENT 10°C B.G, BW
SUN. WKS
MAX 12°C MIN 9.5°C
- Bluetit 2   Blackbird 2
- Greenfinch 3   Starling 4
- Chaffinch 3   Great tit 2
- Blackcap ✻   Collared dove 3
- Siskin 2   Dunnock
- Coal tit
- Magpie
- Wren
- Robin

27th
CURRENT 9.5°C
MAX 11.5°C MIN 2.5°C
- Dunnock
- Bluetit 2
- Blackbird 2
- Collared dove 2
- Chaffinch (M)(F)
- Robin
- Greenfinch ♂♀7
- Starling 2

28th
CURRENT 3.5°C
MAX   MIN 1.5°C
- Starling 2
- Coal tit
- Greenfinch ♂♀8
- Chaffinch ♂♀ (F)(M) 7
- Collared dove 23
- Bluetit 2
- Blackbird 2(4)
- Robin.,
- High winds

26th
Fine, Bright   last shower
- Collared dove 2   Coal tit
- Goldfinch 2   Robin
- Chaffinch
- Bluetit 2
- Blackbird
- Greenfinch ♂♀8
- Dunnock 2
- Siskin
- Starling 2

27th
- Greenfinch ♂4
- Blackbird 2
- Dunnock
- Chaffinch 4
- Bluetit

To London

28th

To Switzerland

Blue tit

JANUARY

YEAR 1 CURRENT 9.5°C 29th	CURRENT 11.5°C 30th	CURRENT 13.5°C 17 31st
MAX 13.5°C MIN 6°C	MAX 13.5°C MIN 4°C	MAX 13.5°C MIN 5.5°C
Dunnock		
Bluetit		
GRASMERE ——————————————————————————————————⟶		

YEAR 2 CURRENT 3°C 29th	CURRENT -1.5°C 30th	CURRENT -3.5°C 31st
MAX 5°C MIN -1.5°C	MAX 6°C MIN -5°C	MAX 2°C MIN -0.5°C
Collared dove 2	Greenfinch 3	Collared dove 2 Great tit 2
Greenfinch 4	Chaffinch (MF) 2	Starling 310 Collared dove
Bluetit 2	Collared dove 3	Robin
Coal tit	Bluetit 2	Blackbird
Chaffinch (M) 2	Starling 56	Dunnock
Blackbird 3	Robin	Chaffinch 3
Dunnock 2	Dunnock	Bluetit 2
Robin	Blackbird	Greenfinch 45
Starling (WINDY)	Great tit	

YEAR 3 29th	30th	31st

JANUARY

Crossbills can be sitting on eggs by the end of January. This extraordinary behaviour is an example of how adaptable birds can be. The pine seeds on which they feed are at their most plentiful throughout the winter months and by nesting early, crossbills can take advantage of this dependable food supply for their hungry youngsters and ensure breeding success.

Crossbills

FEBRUARY CHECKLIST

YEAR	1	2	3
DIVERS			
Red-throated diver			
Black-throated diver			
Great Northern diver			
GREBES			
Little grebe			
Great crested grebe			
Red-necked grebe			
Slavonian grebe			
Black-necked grebe			
SHEARWATERS			
Fulmar			
Cory's shearwater			
Great shearwater			
Sooty shearwater			
Manx shearwater			
Mediterranean shearwater			
STORM PETRELS			
Storm petrel			
Leach's petrel			
GANNETS			
Gannet			
CORMORANTS			
Cormorant			
Shag			
HERONS			
Bittern			
Night heron			
Little egret			
Great white egret			
Grey heron			
Purple heron			
IBISES			
Spoonbill			
DUCKS			
Mute swan			
Bewick's swan			
Whooper swan			
Bean goose			
Pink-footed goose			
White-fronted goose			
Greylag goose			
Snow goose			
Canada goose			
Barnacle goose			
Brent goose			
Egyptian goose			
Shelduck			
Mandarin			
Wigeon			
American wigeon			
Gadwall			
Teal			
Mallard			
Pintail			
Garganey			
Shoveler			
Red-crested pochard			

YEAR	1	2	3
DUCKS (cont.)			
Pochard			
Ring-necked duck			
Ferruginous duck			
Tufted duck			
Scaup			
Eider			
King eider			
Long-tailed duck			
Common scoter			
Surf scoter			
Velvet scoter			
Goldeneye			
Smew			
Red-breasted merganser			
Goosander			
Ruddy duck			
HAWKS			
Honey buzzard			
Black kite			
Red kite			
White-tailed eagle			
Marsh harrier			
Hen harrier			
Montagu's harrier			
Goshawk			
Sparrowhawk			
Buzzard			
Rough-legged buzzard			
Golden eagle			
OSPREYS			
Osprey			
FALCONS			
Kestrel			
Red-footed falcon			
Merlin			
Hobby			
Peregrine			
GROUSE			
Red grouse			
Ptarmigan			
Black grouse			
Capercaillie			
PHEASANTS			
Red-legged partridge			
Grey partridge			
Quail			
Pheasant			
Golden pheasant			
Lady Amherst's pheasant			
RAILS			
Water rail			
Spotted crake			
Corncrake			
Moorhen			
Coot			
CRANES			
Crane			

YEAR	1	2	3
OYSTERCATCHERS			
Oystercatcher			
AVOCETS			
Black-winged stilt			
Avocet			
THICK-KNEES			
Stone curlew			
PLOVERS			
Little ringed plover			
Ringed plover			
Kentish plover			
Dotterel			
Golden plover			
Grey plover			
Lapwing			
Turnstone			
SANDPIPERS			
Knot			
Sanderling			
Little stint			
Temminck's stint			
White-rumped sandpiper			
Pectoral sandpiper			
Curlew sandpiper			
Purple sandpiper			
Dunlin			
Buff-breasted sandpiper			
Ruff			
Jack snipe			
Snipe			
Woodcock			
Black-tailed godwit			
Bar-tailed godwit			
Whimbrel			
Curlew			
Spotted redshank			
Redshank			
Marsh sandpiper			
Greenshank			
Green sandpiper			
Wood sandpiper			
Common sandpiper			
PHALAROPES			
Red-necked phalarope			
Grey phalarope			
SKUAS			
Pomarine skua			
Arctic skua			
Long-tailed skua			
Great skua			
GULLS			
Mediterranean gull			
Little gull			
Sabine's gull			
Black-headed gull			
Ring-billed gull			
Common gull			
Lesser black-backed gull			

YEAR	1	2	3
GULLS (cont.)			
Herring gull			
Iceland gull			
Glaucous gull			
Great black-backed gull			
Kittiwake			
Sandwich tern			
Roseate tern			
Common tern			
Arctic tern			
Little tern			
Black tern			
White-winged black tern			
AUKS			
Guillemot			
Razorbill			
Black guillemot			
Little auk			
Puffin			
PIGEONS			
Rock dove			
Stock dove			
Wood-pigeon	✓	✓	
Collared dove	✓	✓	
Turtle dove			
PARROTS			
Ring-necked parakeet			
CUCKOOS			
Cuckoo			
BARN OWLS			
Barn owl			
OWLS			
Snowy owl			
Little owl			
Tawny owl			
Long-eared owl			
Short-eared owl			
NIGHTJARS			
Nightjar			
SWIFTS			
Swift			
Alpine swift			
KINGFISHERS			
Kingfisher			
BEE-EATERS			
Bee-eater			
HOOPOES			
Hoopoe			
WOODPECKERS			
Wryneck			
Green woodpecker			
Great spotted woodpecker.			
Lesser spotted woodpecker			
LARKS			
Short-toed lark			
Woodlark			
Skylark			
Shore lark			

YEAR	1	2	3
SWALLOWS			
Sand martin			
Swallow			
House martin			
PIPITS			
Richard's pipit			
Tawny pipit			
Tree pipit			
Meadow pipit			
Red-throated pipit			
Rock pipit			
Water pipit			
Yellow wagtail			
Grey wagtail			
Pied wagtail			
WAXWINGS			
Waxwing			
DIPPERS			
Dipper			
WRENS			
Wren	✓		✓
ACCENTORS			
Dunnock	✓	✓	✓
THRUSHES			
Robin	✓	✓	✓
Nightingale			
Bluethroat			
Black redstart			
Redstart			
Whinchat			
Stonechat			
Wheatear			
Ring ouzel			
Blackbird	✓	✓	✓
Fieldfare			
Song thrush			
Redwing			
Mistle thrush			
FLYCATCHERS			
Cetti's warbler			
Grasshopper warbler			
Savi's warbler			
Aquatic warbler			
Sedge warbler			
Marsh warbler			
Reed warbler			
Icterine warbler			
Melodious warbler			
Dartford warbler			
Subalpine warbler			
Barred warbler			
Lesser whitethroat			
Whitethroat			
Garden warbler			
Blackcap			
Pallas's warbler			
Yellow-browed warbler			
Wood warbler			

YEAR	1	2	3
FLYCATCHERS (*cont.*)			
Chiffchaff			
Willow warbler			
Goldcrest			
Firecrest			
Spotted flycatcher			
Red-breasted flycatcher			
Pied flycatcher			
REEDLINGS			
Bearded tit			
TITMICE			
Long-tailed tit			
Marsh tit			
Willow tit			
Crested tit			
Coal tit	✓		✓
Blue tit	✓	✓	✓
Great tit	✓	✓	✓
NUTHATCHES			
Nuthatch			
CREEPERS			
Treecreeper			
ORIOLES			
Golden oriole			
SHRIKES			
Red-backed shrike			
Great Grey shrike			
Woodchat shrike			
CROWS			
Jay	✓		
Magpie			✓
Chough			
Jackdaw			
Rook			
Carrion crow			✓
Raven			
STARLINGS			
Starling	✓	✓	✓
SPARROWS			
House sparrow			✓
Tree sparrow			
BUNTINGS			
Lapland bunting			
Snow bunting			
Yellowhammer			
Cirl bunting			
Ortolan bunting			
Little bunting			
Reed bunting			
Corn bunting			
FINCHES			
Chaffinch	✓	✓	✓
Brambling		✓	✓
Serin			
Greenfinch	✓	✓	✓
Goldfinch			✓
Siskin	✓	✓	✓
Linnet			

YEAR	1	2	3
FINCHES (*cont.*)			
Twite			
Redpoll			
Arctic redpoll			
Crossbill			
Scottish crossbill			
Scarlet rosefinch			
Bullfinch	✓		
Hawfinch			

NON-LISTED SIGHTINGS

Waxwings are irregular winter visitors to our shores from Scandinavia and Russia. They feed on rowan, hawthorn, and holly berries in the countryside. Often they invade town parks and gardens, where they strip the fruits of ornamental shrubs such as pyracantha and cotoneaster.

FEBRUARY

YEAR 1 CURRENT ~~17°C~~ 13·8°C 1st	CURRENT 13°C 2nd	CURRENT 11°C 9am 3rd	CURRENT 8.30. 4°C 4th
MAX 13.5°C MIN. 10°C	MAX 14.5°C MIN 8°C	Sunday WK6 MAX 12°C MIN 2°C	MAX 14°C MIN 4°C
Bluetit	Blackbird	Blackbird 3	Blackbird
	Bluetit	Bluetit 2	Bluetit
		Dunnock 2	Collared dove 2
		Robin 1	Dunnock 2
GRASMERE			

YEAR 2 CURRENT 3.5°C 1st	CURRENT 2.5°C 2nd	CURRENT 0.5°C 3rd	CURRENT 0°C 4th
MAX 9.5°C MIN 2°C	WK6 Sun. MAX 5°C MIN 0°C	MAX 5°C MIN −1.5°C	MAX MIN
Bluetit 3 Bullfinch (MF) 2	Blackbird Goldfinch 3	Bluetit 2 Dunnock	Blackbird 2
Blackbird 3 Wood pigeon	Starling 4	Greenfinch 2·3 Magpie	Bluetit 2
Dunnock Collared dove 2	Chaffinch 2·3	Starling 3·6·3	Chaffinch 2
Robin	Bluetit 2	Blackbird	Greenfinch 2
Chaffinch 2	Greenfinch 3·7	Chaffinch 2	Siskin 3
Greenfinch 3	Great tit	Blackbird 2·3	
Starling 3	Dunnock 2	Robin	
Great tit	Robin	Collared dove 2 SNOW	
Siskin	Collared dove 2	~~WHITBARROW~~ VILLAGE	SNOW ———

YEAR 3 1st	2nd	3rd	4th

FEBRUARY

CURRENT 8am. 8.5°C 5th	CURRENT 8.30AM 6°C 6th	CURRENT 8.50m. 5°C 7th
MAX 12°C MIN 3.5°C	MAX 8.5° MIN 2°C	MAX 11.5°C MIN 4.5°C
Bluetit 2	Bluetit 2	Bluetit
Collared dove	Collared dove 2	Blackbird
Blackbird 2	Greenfinch	Collared dove 2
		Magpie

5th	CURRENT 6pm. 8.5°C 6th	7th
	MAX 10.5°C MIN 4.5°C	MAX 8.5°C MIN 7.5°C
—	—	RETURN FROM W.V.

5th	6th	7th
		Collared dove 2
		Chaffinch
		Greenfinch &7
		Blackbird
		Bluetit 2
		Starling
		Robin
	Return from Switzerland	

ADDITIONAL NOTES:

* 1st this winter

A drake smew in winter is a beautiful sight, instantly recognisable by its contrasing black and white plumage and drooping crest. Females and immature drakes are more sombre, with chestnut brown heads and grey upper parts they are often referred to as 'redheads'.

Drake smew

FEBRUARY

YEAR 1

8th — Current 8.50am 10.5°C MAX 12.5°C MIN 6°C	9th — Current 9.15am 7.5°C MAX 12.5°C MIN 3.5°C	10th — CURRENT 5.10PM 10°C Sunday wk7 MAX 12°C MIN 10°C	11th — CURRENT 8.50am 10°C MAX 12.5°C MIN 7°C
Dunnock 2	Blackbird 2		Woodpigeon
Robin	Bluetit 2		Blackbird
Bluetit 2	Dunnock 2		Bluetit 2
Blackbird 2			Coal tit
			Dunnock 2

HULL ⟶ HULL

YEAR 2

8th — CURRENT 8.5°C MAX 12.5°C MIN 5.5°C	9th — CURRENT 5.5°C SUN wk7 MAX 15°C MIN −3.5°C	10th — CURRENT −1.5°C MAX 10°C MIN −1.5°C	11th — CURRENT 6.5°C MAX 16°C MIN 0°C
Chaffinch 3 Coal tit	Starling 2,3,4,8 Dunnock	Blackbird 2 Coal tit	Greenfinch 4 Wren
Brambling Blackbird	Bluetit 2 Wren	Bluetit 2	Bluetit 2
Siskin 2,3 Robin	Greenfinch 3,4 Blackbird	Starling 3	Chaffinch
Collared dove 2	Chaffinch 2 Longtailed tit	Chaffinch	Collared dove
Starling 5	Great tit 2 Siskin 2	Greenfinch 3	Dunnock 2
Bluetit 2	Collared dove 2	Robin	Blackbird
Dunnock 3	Robin	Dunnock 2	Starling 4
Greenfinch 2,4	Brambling	Collared dove 2	Great tit 2
Great tit 2	Magpie 2	Siskin 2	Robin

YEAR 3

8th — SUN wk7	9th	10th	11th
Collared dove 2 Siskins 4	Siskins 3	Starling 4	Starling 2
Greenfinch 2,4	Greenfinch 2	Greenfinch 4,5,7	Chaffinch
Chaffinch 2	Bluetit	Bluetit 2	Bluetit
Bluetit 2	Blackbird	Chaffinch 2	Greenfinch 2
Blackbird		Dunnock 2	Dunnock
Dunnock		Blackbird	Blackbird
Great tit		Collared dove	Siskin 2
Coal tit		Siskin 3,4	Robin
Goldfinch			H.Sparrow

FEBRUARY

CURRENT 8.30am 8.5°C **12th**	CURRENT 8.45am 6°C **13th**	CURRENT 9am 5.5°C **14th**
MAX 12°C MIN 4°C	MAX 8°C MIN 0°C	MAX 13.5°C MIN 1°C
Blackbird	Blackbird.	Greenfinch
Bluetit 2		Bluetit 2
Collared dove 2		
Dunnock.		
	OTLEY LEEDS	

CURRENT 2°C **12th**	CURRENT 2.5°C **13th**	CURRENT -3°C **14th**
MAX 16°C MIN 0°C	MAX 8°C MIN -4.5°C	MAX 11°C MIN -4.5°C
Bluetit 2 Great tit 2	Bluetit 2	Siskin 2
Starling 16 Coal tit	Greenfinch 36	Starling 2
Greenfinch 24 Blackbird (M)	Chaffinch 2	Chaffinch 23
Dunnock 23	Collared dove 2	Bluetit 2
Chaffinch 2	Siskin	Collared dove 2
Brambling 2	Blackbird	Robin
Robin	Starling	Greenfinch 2
Collared dove		Linnet (F)
Siskin 2	(Gym, Anna, Leeds LG1)	

12th	**13th**	**14th**
Blackbird 2 Collared dove 2	Goldfinch 2	Bluetit 23 Collared dove
Bluetit 2	Bluetit	Chaffinch 23 Goldfinch
Siskin 23	Greenfinch 4	Blackbird 2 Crow
Robin	Chaffinch 23	Greenfinch 23741
Starling 579	Starling	Dunnock 2
Chaffinch 2	Collared dove	Siskin 23
Greenfinch 25	Siskin 3	Starling 5
Dunnock 2	Dunnock 2	Great tit
+ Sparrow 3		Coal tit

ADDITIONAL NOTES:

The siskin is now a regular winter visitor to peanut bags in our gardens. It used to be found only in the pine forests of the Scottish Highlands. Modern conifer plantations provide siskins with food in the form of pine and spruce seeds, which has allowed them to increase their breeding range considerably.

Siskin

FEBRUARY

YEAR 1 2001 CURRENT max 5°C — 15th	CURRENT 2.5°C (8.25am) — 16th	Start of Year 2001 — 17th	18th
MAX 12.5°C MIN 1.5°C	MAX 16°C MIN 2.5°C		
Blackbird 2	Blackbird	Bluetit	Bluetit 2
Bluetit 1	Bluetit 2	Blackbird	Blackbird 3
Coal tit	Coal tit	Collared dove	Collared Dove 2
	Starling 3	Jay (unusual)	Robin
	Greenfinch		Dunnock 2
	Dunnock 2		
	Collared dove 2		

YEAR 2 CURRENT -2°C — 15th	CURRENT 2°C SUN WK3 — 16th	SUN WK8 2002 YR2 CURRENT 9.5°C — 17th	CURRENT 3.5°C — 18th
MAX 18.5°C MIN -2.5°C	MAX 10°C MIN -3.5°C	MAX 16°C MIN 2°C	MAX 16°C MIN 2°C
Bluetit	Bluetit 2 Coal tit	Starlings 5	
Collared dove 2	Greenfinch 7?8	Greenfinch 2	
Linnet	Magpie	Bluetit 2	
Siskin	Chaffinch	Dunnock 2	
Greenfinch 2	Starling 35	Blackbird	
	Robin	Robin	
	Collared dove 2	Chaffinch (F)	
	Siskin 2		
	Blackbird	TO GRASMERE	GRASMERE

YEAR 3 SUN WK8 — 15th	16th	YR3 CURRENT 0.5°C with windchill -2°C all day — 17th	CURRENT -0.5°C with windchill below 0°C all day — 18th
		MAX 13°C MIN -5.0°C	MAX 17°C MIN -2.5°C
Chaffinch 3 H Sparrow 3	Starling 3	Siskin 2?3 Bullfinch (M)	Bluetit 2
Siskin 3 Dunnock 2	Blackbird 2	Chaffinch (M F) 2	Dunnock 2
Bluetit	Chaffinch	Robin	Chaffinch 2
Starling	Bluetit	Starling 5	Starling 5
Collared dove	Greenfinch 2	Dunnock 2	Blackbird
Blackbird 2	Collared dove 2	Blackbird	Greenfinch 7?8
Goldfinch		H Sparrow	Siskin 3?4
Robin		Bluetit	Collared dove 2?3
Greenfinch 2?3	See next Book Cont.	Greenfinch 2	Wren

FEBRUARY

16" Swarms of large insects around G.finch
on top of tall leylandii. Drone it away, stayed
circling for about further minute, not midges
Since Feb 7th bluetits flying in & out of
nesting box on regular basis.
Robin singing from higher in tree 17th
Greenfinch singing top of tall leylandii from
16th

2001 **19th**	**20th**	**21st**
Blackbird	Blackbird 2	Bluetit 2
Bluetit 2	Bluetit 2	Blackbird 2
Greenfinch 2	Collared Dove 2	Wren
Dunnock 2	Siskin	Robin
Collared Doves 2	Dunnock	Dunnock
	Wren	Greenfinch 2

CURRENT 5.5°C **19th**	CURRENT 4.5°C **20th**	CURRENT 8 3°C **21st**
MAX 16°C MIN 2°C	MAX 8C MIN 0°C	MAX 10°C MIN 2.5°C

At this time of year, few birds are heard singing but one notable exception is the wren. With a voice which always seems incredibly loud for such a tiny bird, wrens brighten many a grey winter day.

GRASMERE	GRASMERE	GRASMERE
CURRENT - 0.5°C **19th**	CURRENT 0°C **20th**	CURRENT 2.5°C **21st**
MAX 12°C MIN -1.5°C	MAX 10.5°C MIN 0°C	MAX 13°C MIN 0°C
Blackbird 2 Chaffinch 2	Siskin 235	Greenfinch 3
Robin Collared dove 2	Bluetit 2	Siskin 2
Bluetit 2	Dunnock 23	Starling 3
Dunnock 3	Great tit 2	Bluetit
Siskin 2	Chaffinch	Blackbird 2
Starling 863	Collared dove 2	H. Sparrow (M)
Greenfinch 4	Greenfinch 4	Collared dove 2
H. Sparrow (M)	Starling 7	Goldfinch 2
Great tit 2	Robin	Chaffinch 2

Wren

FEBRUARY

YEAR 1 2001 22nd	23rd	24th	25th
Robin	Robin	Magpie	
Dunnock	Dunnock 2		
	Blackbird 2		
	Coal Tit		
	Blue Tit 2		
	Collared Dove		

YEAR 2 CURRENT 5.5°C 22nd MAX 10°C MIN 0°C	CURRENT 0°C 23rd MAX 6°C MIN -0.5°C	CURRENT 2°C SUN. WK. 2. 24th MAX 10°C MIN -0.5°C	CURRENT 4.5°C 25th MAX 11°C MIN 3.5°C
	Dunnock 2	Bluetit 2	Magpie
	Chaffinch (F)	Great tit	Blackbird
	Collared dove 2	Robin	
	Blackbird	Dunnock 2.	
GALES	HIGH WINDS & SNOW		
GRASMERE	RETURN GRASMERE		

YEAR 3 CURRENT 2.5°C 22nd MAX 16.5°C MIN -0.5°C	CURRENT 4°C SUN. WK 9 23rd MAX MIN	24th	25th
Bluetit 2 Chaffinch 23	Bluetit 2 Great tit		
Woodpigeon Dunnock 2	Siskin 5		
Blackbird Great tit 2	Starling 2		
Greenfinch 4 Goldfinch 2	Blackbird		
Crow Bullfinch (M)	Chaffinch 3		
Siskin 3 Robin	Bullfinch (F!!) Murray (MF) 2		
Starling 3 Wren	Greenfinch 2		
Blackbird	Robin		
Collared dove	Grasmere.	Grasmere	Grasmere

FEBRUARY

	26th		27th		28th

CURRENT 4°C 26th	CURRENT 4·5°C 27th	CURRENT 4°C 28th
MAX 9·5°C MIN 1·5°C	MAX 11·5°C MIN 1·5°C	MAX 8°C MIN 0°C
Greenfinch	Magpie	Blackbird 2
Bluetit 2		Greenfinch
Collared dove		Starlings 4
Chaffinch -		Chaffinch (F2)
Blackbird		Dunnock 2
Dunnock 2.		Bluetit 2
Magpie 2.		Collared dove
	F. A. + Otley	Magpie (snow)

	26th		27th		28th
				MAX 20·5°C MIN 0°C	
Grasmere		Grasmere		Grasmere,	

2001 ADDITIONAL NOTES:

Bluetits have regularly flown in & out of nesting box since beginning of this month (TA) a month earlier than last year

Heavy snowfalls can make life very difficult for many birds. Barn owls in particular can encounter problems in finding mice and voles under a thick layer of snow. It is at this time of year that they can most often be seen in broad daylight, taking full advantage of snow-free days to hunt for food.

Barn owl

MARCH CHECKLIST

YEAR	1	2	3
DIVERS			
Red-throated diver			
Black-throated diver			
Great Northern diver			
GREBES			
Little grebe			
Great crested grebe			
Red-necked grebe			
Slavonian grebe			
Black-necked grebe			
SHEARWATERS			
Fulmar			
Cory's shearwater			
Great shearwater			
Sooty shearwater			
Manx shearwater			
Mediterranean shearwater			
STORM PETRELS			
Storm petrel			
Leach's petrel			
GANNETS			
Gannet			
CORMORANTS			
Cormorant			
Shag			
HERONS			
Bittern			
Night heron			
Little egret			
Great white egret			
Grey heron			
Purple heron			
IBISES			
Spoonbill			
DUCKS			
Mute swan			
Bewick's swan			
Whooper swan			
Bean goose			
Pink-footed goose			
White-fronted goose			
Greylag goose			
Snow goose			
Canada goose			
Barnacle goose			
Brent goose			
Egyptian goose			
Shelduck			
Mandarin			
Wigeon			
American wigeon			
Gadwall			
Teal			
Mallard			
Pintail			
Garganey			
Shoveler			
Red-crested pochard			

YEAR	1	2	3
DUCKS (*cont.*)			
Pochard			
Ring-necked duck			
Ferruginous duck			
Tufted duck			
Scaup			
Eider			
King eider			
Long-tailed duck			
Common scoter			
Surf scoter			
Velvet scoter			
Goldeneye			
Smew			
Red-breasted merganser			
Goosander			
Ruddy duck			
HAWKS			
Honey buzzard			
Black kite			
Red kite			
White-tailed eagle			
Marsh harrier			
Hen harrier			
Montagu's harrier			
Goshawk			
Sparrowhawk			
Buzzard			
Rough-legged buzzard			
Golden eagle			
OSPREYS			
Osprey			
FALCONS			
Kestrel			
Red-footed falcon			
Merlin			
Hobby			
Peregrine			
GROUSE			
Red grouse			
Ptarmigan			
Black grouse			
Capercaillie			
PHEASANTS			
Red-legged partridge			
Grey partridge			
Quail			
Pheasant			
Golden pheasant			
Lady Amherst's pheasant			
RAILS			
Water rail			
Spotted crake			
Corncrake			
Moorhen			
Coot			
CRANES			
Crane			

YEAR	1	2	3
OYSTERCATCHERS			
Oystercatcher			
AVOCETS			
Black-winged stilt			
Avocet			
THICK-KNEES			
Stone curlew			
PLOVERS			
Little ringed plover			
Ringed plover			
Kentish plover			
Dotterel			
Golden plover			
Grey plover			
Lapwing			
Turnstone			
SANDPIPERS			
Knot			
Sanderling			
Little stint			
Temminck's stint			
White-rumped sandpiper			
Pectoral sandpiper			
Curlew sandpiper			
Purple sandpiper			
Dunlin			
Buff-breasted sandpiper			
Ruff			
Jack snipe			
Snipe			
Woodcock			
Black-tailed godwit			
Bar-tailed godwit			
Whimbrel			
Curlew			
Spotted redshank			
Redshank			
Marsh sandpiper			
Greenshank			
Green sandpiper			
Wood sandpiper			
Common sandpiper			
PHALAROPES			
Red-necked phalarope			
Grey phalarope			
SKUAS			
Pomarine skua			
Arctic skua			
Long-tailed skua			
Great skua			
GULLS			
Mediterranean gull			
Little gull			
Sabine's gull			
Black-headed gull			
Ring-billed gull			
Common gull			
Lesser black-backed gull			

YEAR	1	2	3
GULLS (*cont.*)			
Herring gull			
Iceland gull			
Glaucous gull			
Great black-backed gull			
Kittiwake			
Sandwich tern			
Roseate tern			
Common tern			
Arctic tern			
Little tern			
Black tern			
White-winged black tern			
AUKS			
Guillemot			
Razorbill			
Black guillemot			
Little auk			
Puffin			
PIGEONS			
Rock dove			
Stock dove			
Wood-pigeon	✓	✓	✓
Collared dove	✓	✓	✓
Turtle dove			
PARROTS			
Ring-necked parakeet			
CUCKOOS			
Cuckoo			
BARN OWLS			
Barn owl			
OWLS			
Snowy owl			
Little owl			
Tawny owl			
Long-eared owl			
Short-eared owl			
NIGHTJARS			
Nightjar			
SWIFTS			
Swift			
Alpine swift			
KINGFISHERS			
Kingfisher			
BEE-EATERS			
Bee-eater			
HOOPOES			
Hoopoe			
WOODPECKERS			
Wryneck			
Green woodpecker			
Great spotted woodpecker.			
Lesser spotted woodpecker			
LARKS			
Short-toed lark			
Woodlark			
Skylark			
Shore lark			

YEAR	1	2	3
SWALLOWS			
Sand martin			
Swallow			
House martin			
PIPITS			
Richard's pipit			
Tawny pipit			
Tree pipit			
Meadow pipit			
Red-throated pipit			
Rock pipit			
Water pipit			
Yellow wagtail			
Grey wagtail			
Pied wagtail			
WAXWINGS			
Waxwing			
DIPPERS			
Dipper			
WRENS			
Wren	✓	✓	✓
ACCENTORS			
Dunnock	✓	✓	✓
THRUSHES			
Robin	✓	✓	✓
Nightingale			
Bluethroat			
Black redstart			
Redstart			
Whinchat			
Stonechat			
Wheatear			
Ring ouzel			
Blackbird	✓	✓	
Fieldfare			
Song thrush			
Redwing			
Mistle thrush			
FLYCATCHERS			
Cetti's warbler			
Grasshopper warbler			
Savi's warbler			
Aquatic warbler			
Sedge warbler			
Marsh warbler			
Reed warbler			
Icterine warbler			
Melodious warbler			
Dartford warbler			
Subalpine warbler			
Barred warbler			
Lesser whitethroat			
Whitethroat			
Garden warbler			
Blackcap	✓	✓	
Pallas's warbler			
Yellow-browed warbler			
Wood warbler			

YEAR	1	2	3
FLYCATCHERS (*cont.*)			
Chiffchaff			
Willow warbler			
Goldcrest			
Firecrest			
Spotted flycatcher			
Red-breasted flycatcher			
Pied flycatcher			
REEDLINGS			
Bearded tit			
TITMICE			
Long-tailed tit			✓
Marsh tit			
Willow tit			
Crested tit			
Coal tit	✓	✓	✓
Blue tit	✓	✓	✓
Great tit	✓		✓
NUTHATCHES			
Nuthatch			
CREEPERS			
Treecreeper			
ORIOLES			
Golden oriole			
SHRIKES			
Red-backed shrike			
Great Grey shrike			
Woodchat shrike			
CROWS			
Jay			
Magpie	✓	✓	✓
Chough			
Jackdaw	✓		
Rook			
Carrion crow	✓	✓	✓
Raven			
STARLINGS			
Starling	✓	✓	✓
SPARROWS			
House sparrow			
Tree sparrow			
BUNTINGS			
Lapland bunting			
Snow bunting			
Yellowhammer			
Cirl bunting			
Ortolan bunting			
Little bunting			
Reed bunting			
Corn bunting			
FINCHES			
Chaffinch	✓	✓	✓
Brambling			✓
Serin			
Greenfinch	✓	✓	✓
Goldfinch		✓	✓
Siskin		✓	✓
Linnet			

YEAR	1	2	3
FINCHES (*cont.*)			
Twite			
Redpoll			✓
Arctic redpoll			
Crossbill			
Scottish crossbill			
Scarlet rosefinch			
Bullfinch	✓	✓	✓
Hawfinch			

NON-LISTED SIGHTINGS (19)

The first wheatears arrive in the south of the country in the middle of March, after spending the winter in Africa. Unlike the male illustrated here, females have brown upperparts but both sexes can easily be recognised by their distinctive tail pattern.

MARCH

YEAR 1	1st	2nd	3rd	Start of Year 2001	4th
				Bluetit 3
				Blackbird 2
				Dunnock 3
				Magpie
				Robin
				Collared Dove 2

YEAR 2 CURRENT 1·5°C 1st MAX 11·5°C MIN −1°C	CURRENT 3·5°C 2nd MAX 11·5°C MIN −1°C	Sun. Wk10 CURRENT 7°C (9·4) 3rd MAX 12°C MIN 7°C	CURRENT 8°C 4th MAX 9·5°C MIN 2·5°C
Blackbird	Greenfinch 2	Crow	Magpie
Bluetit 2	Woodpigeon	Bluetit 2	Great tit
	Bluetit 2	Robin	Bluetit 2
	Blackbird (E)	Chaffinch (F)(F) 2	Blackbird
	Magpie	Blackbird 2	Greenfinch 2
	Robin	Coal tit	Starling 5
		Greenfinch 4	Woodpigeon
		Collared dove	
F A @ Phillipa's	Helmsley		

YEAR 3 CURRENT 3pm 10°C 1st MAX 13°C MIN 2·5°C	CURRENT 6°C 2nd Sun Wk10 MAX 19·5°C MIN 0°C	CURRENT 3°C 3rd MAX 12·5°C MIN 3°C	CURRENT 8°C 4th MAX 14°C MIN 7°C
Siskin Goldfinch 2	Siskin 5 Wren	Bluetit 2	Bluetit
Chaffinch	Bluetit 2 Blackbird	Siskin 3	Starling 8
Greenfinch	Collared dove 2 Bullfinch (M-F) 2	Starling 4	Blackbird 2
Blackbird	Greenfinch 6	Greenfinch 2	Greenfinch 4
Collared dove	Brambling	Collared dove 2	Chaffinch
Bluetit 2	Chaffinch 2	Chaffinch 2	Bullfinch 2
Starling 3	Dunnock 2		~~Blackbird~~
Dunnock	Starling 33		Collared dove 2
Return from Grasmere	Robin		

MARCH

	5th		6th		7th
Bluetit 2		Blackbird ♀3		Greenfinch 3	
Blackbird 2		Dunnock 1		Starling 6	
Chaffinch		Blue tit 2		Bluetit 2	
Crow				Great Tit	
Dunnock 2.				Blackbird	
				Dunnock	
		(Out most of day)		Saw bluetit with moss go into nesting box	

CURRENT 5°C 5th	CURRENT 9°C 6th	CURRENT 6.5°C 7th
MAX 11°C MIN 4.5°C	MAX 12°C MIN 6.5°C	MAX 11.5°C MIN 5°C
Blackbird 2	Bluetit 2	Bluetit 3
Robin	Blackbird	Dunnock 2
Magpie 5	Greenfinch 4	
Starling 2	Robin	
Bluetit 3		
Chaffinch & (MFF) 3		
Greenfinch 2		
Coaltit	(gales) F Abbey (V. windy)	

CURRENT 10.5°C 5th	CURRENT 6.5°C 6th	CURRENT 7.5°C 7th
MAX 12.5°C MIN 3.5°C	MAX 20°C MIN 2.5°C	MAX 14°C MIN 3°C
Bluetit 2 Robin 3	Collared dove 2 Crow	Starling 5 Redpoll Ⓜ
Blackbird 2 Collared dove 2	Bluetit 2	Greenfinch 5 Robin
Greenfinch 3	Dunnock 2	Chaffinch & 3 Brambling
Chaffinch 2	Greenfinch 2	Bluetit 2
Siskin 2	Starling 3	Siskin 2
Wren	Chaffinch 2	Blackbird
Chaffinch 2	Siskin	Dunnock 2
Bullfinch (F)	Blackbird	Wren
Dunnock 3	Wren	Collared dove

One of the first summer visitors to arrive in Britain is the sand martin. Having flown north from equatorial West Africa, these intrepid tourists return to their nest sites to prepare for the breeding season in mid-May.

Sand martins

MARCH

2001

YEAR 1 2001 8th	9th	10th	SUN. 11th
Dunnock 2			Bluetit 2 Coal Tit
Bluetit 2			Blackbird 2
Greenfinch 1			Robin
			Starling
			Dunnock
			Gt. Tit
	Helmsley	Helmsley	Greenfinch 3
	Scarborough.	Scarborough.	Collared Dove
			Magpie

YEAR 2 CURRENT 11·5°C 8th	CURRENT 5·5°C 9th	SUN. WR 11 CURRENT 7·5°C 10th	CURRENT 11th
MAX 13°C MIN 2°C	MAX 10·5°C MIN 1°C	MAX MIN	MAX 13°C MIN 0°C
Starling 3	Bluetit 2	Starlings 5	Blackbird 2
Magpie 4	Collared dove	Bluetit 2	Bluetit 2
Bluetit	Greenfinch 2	Dunnock 2	Magpie 2
Blackbird	Blackbird	Chaffinch (2F)	Robin
Greenfinch 2	Starling	Blackbird	
Dunnock 2	Dunnock 2	Collared dove 2	
Chaffinch (M)(F)			
	Helmsley (snow/slush)		

YEAR 3 CURRENT 5·5°C 8th	CURRENT 11°C COLD WIND SUN WR 11 9th	CURRENT 10°C 10th	CURRENT 9·5°C 11th
MAX 12·5°C MIN 4·5°C	MAX 26°C MIN 6·5°C	MAX 15·5°C MIN 8·5°C	MAX 15·5°C MIN 3·5°C
Greenfinch 6 Wren	Greenfinch 6 Dunnock 2	Collared dove	Siskin
Blackbird 2	Crow Great tit	Siskin 2	Bluetit 2
Starling 3 Collared dove 2	Starling 4	Bluetit 2	Great tit
Bluetit 2	Blackbird	Chaffinch 2	Dunnock 2
Chaffinch 2	Bluetit 2	Dunnock 2	Chaffinch 3
Dunnock 2	Chaffinch 2	Blackbird 2	Robin
Bullfinch (M)	Siskin 2	Greenfinch 4	Greenfinch 2
Robin	Wren	Brambling	Starling 2
Siskin 2	Collared dove 3	Robin	Collared dove

MARCH

	12th	13th	14th
	Bluetit	Blackbird 2	2 Collared doves
	Collared Dove	Greenfinch 2	Bluetit
	Dunnock 2	Robin	
		Bluetit 2	
		Dunnock	
		Wren	

12th	13th	14th
CURRENT 10.5°C	CURRENT 2.5°C	CURRENT 8.5°C
MAX 15°C MIN 0°C	MAX 19°C MIN 0.5°C	MAX 15°C MIN 3°C
Starling 2	Greenfinch 2	Blackbird
Greenfinch 23	Blackbird	Robin
Bluetit 2	Bluetit 3	Bluetit 2
Blackbird	Chaffinch	Greenfinch 235
Dunnock 2		Dunnock 2
Coal tit 2		Starlings 3
		Collared dove
F.A.	F.A.	AMSTERDAM P.M.

12th	13th	14th
CURRENT 4.5°C	CURRENT 6°C	CURRENT 9°C
MAX 14.5°C MIN 1°C	MAX 12°C MIN 4°C	MAX 24°C MIN 0°C
Crow 2	Starling 23 Collared dove 2	Starling 7 Chaffinch
Starling 3	Dunnock 2	Blackbird
Siskin 2	Great tit 2	Bluetit 2
Bluetit 2	Greenfinch 4	Greenfinch 2
Robin	Robin	Collared dove
Chaffinch 3	Bluetit 3	Dunnock 2
Greenfinch 3	Chaffinch 2	Great tit 2
Dunnock 2	Brambling	Robin
Blackbird	Blackbird	Siskin 2

ADDITIONAL NOTES:

March sees the arrival of the chiffchaff; this little member of the warbler family announces its presence by repeatedly singing its own name. Not much of a song by warbler standards admittedly, but a true sign that spring is on the way.

Chiffchaff

MARCH

YEAR 1 2001 — 15th	16th	17th	18th
2 Starlings	Blackbird	Collared dove 2	Bluetit 2
Bluetit	Bluetit 2	Robin	Robin 1
Chaffinch (F)	Dunnock	Bluetit 2	Blackbird 2
2 Collared doves	Robin	Greenfinch	Dunnock
Dunnock	Chaffinch (F)	Blackbird	Chaffinch
	Collared doves 2	Blackcap	Greenfinch
		Chaffinch (M)	Collared dove 2
			Magpie

YEAR 2 CURRENT 7.5°C — 15th MAX 11°C MIN 3°C	CURRENT 10°C — 16th MAX 16.5°C MIN 6°C	CURRENT 8.5°C SUN WK 12 — 17th MAX 19.5°C MIN 4.5°C	CURRENT 10°C — 18th MAX 15°C MIN 4°C
	Bluetit 2	Blackbird	Magpie
	Blackbird Starling	Greenfinch 2	Starling 2
	Greenfinch 3 Black cap	Siskin 2	Bluetit 2
	Dunnock 2	Bluetit 2	Dunnock 2
	Crow	Dunnock	Greenfinch
	Siskin 3	Chaffinch (F)(M)	Blackbird
	Chaffinch	Starling 2	
	Robin		
AMSTERDAM	RETURN AMSTERDAM		

YEAR 3 CURRENT 4°C (Foggy) — 15th MAX 25.5°C MIN -2.5°C	CURRENT 2.5°C SUN WK 12 — 16th MAX 27.5°C MIN 0.5°C	CURRENT 4°C — 17th MAX 26°C MIN 3°C	CURRENT 5°C — 18th MAX 24°C MIN 0°C
Blackbird	Starling 7	Greenfinch 3 Dunnock 2	Blackbird 2 Collared dove 2
Bluetit	Dunnock 2	Bluetit	Bluetit 2 Long tailed tit 4
Goldfinch 2	Greenfinch 2	Great tit	Great tit 2 Magpie
Siskin 2	Great tit	Starling 2	Dunnock 2
Greenfinch 3	Chaffinch 2	Chaffinch 2	Greenfinch 6
Chaffinch 2	Bluetit 2	Brambling	Bullfinch 2
Dunnock	Siskin	Blackbird 2	Chaffinch 2
		Collared dove 2	Starling 6
		Siskin	Red Poll 2

MARCH

	19th	20th	21st
	AMSTERDAM	2 Bluetit	Blackbird (with nesting material)
		Dunnock 2	Bluetit
		Collared dove 2	Robin
		Blackbird	Dunnock
		Robin	Collared Doves 2
		Greenfinch 2	
		Magpie	

2002
16th March. 3 siskins 1st this year +
1 Black cap!
18th March 2003 Redpoll back again
pair of !!

19th	20th	21st
CURRENT 8°C	CURRENT 10.5°C	CURRENT 11.5°C
MAX 13.5°C MIN 6°C	MAX 15.5°C MIN 8.5°C	MAX 16.5°C MIN 9°C
Bluetit 2	Starling 2	Blackbird
Greenfinch	Bluetit 2	Collared dove
Dunnock 2	Dunnock	Bluetit
Chaffinch	Greenfinch 2 3	Magpie
	Blackbird	Starling
	Collared dove	

This is the month to watch out for displaying sparrowhawks as they soar together, prior to nesting. The male is considerably smaller than the female and in good light you can see his blue-grey back and rufous underparts.

19th	20th	21st
CURRENT 3.5°C	CURRENT 4.5°C	CURRENT 10°C
MAX 31.5°C MIN 0°C	MAX 10°C MIN 2.5°C	MAX 28.5°C MIN −1.5°
Greenfinch 2	Starling 2 Robin	Bluetit
Bluetit 3	Greenfinch 5 Brambling 2	Collared dove
Blackbird	Chaffinch 2	Starling 2
Dunnock	Bluetit 2	Blackbird 2
Siskin	Great tit	Dunnock 2
Chaffinch	Blackbird	Greenfinch 2
Starlings 3	Dunnock 2	Chaffinch 2
Collared dove 2	Collared dove 2	
	Siskin	

Sparrowhawks

MARCH

YEAR 1 2001 22nd	23rd	24th	25th
3" of snow a.m.			
2 Starlings	Blackcap	Blackbird 2	Collared dove 2
Bluetit 2	Magpie 2	Robin	Bluetit 2
Greenfinch	Dunnock	Dunnock	Blackbird
Dunnock 2	Robin		Greenfinch 2
Blackbird 2	Bluetit 2		Chaffinch
Robin	Blackbird		Blackcap
Starlings 10	Greenfinch 2		
	Starling	(Helmsley)	

YEAR 2 CURRENT 11°C 22nd	CURRENT 9°C 23rd	SUN WK 13 CURRENT 8.5°C 24th	CURRENT 12°C 25th
MAX 16.5°C MIN 9.5°C	MAX 15.5°C MIN 4.0°C	MAX 15.5°C MIN 7.5°C	MAX 15.5°C MIN 2°C
Bluetit 2	Starling 3	Collared dove	Dunnock
Starling 3	Bluetit	Blackbird 2	Bluetit 2
Dunnock	Dunnock	Bluetit 2	Blackbird 2
Blackbird	Greenfinch	Dunnock	Robin
	Magpie 2	Greenfinch 2	Collared dove
		Chaffinch	Greenfinch
		Bullfinch (M&F)	

YEAR 3 CURRENT 1.5°C 22nd	CURRENT 2°C SUN WK13 23rd	CURRENT 10°C 24th	CURRENT 6°C 25th
MAX 27.5°C MIN −2°C	MAX 30.5° MIN 2°C	MAX 22.5°C MIN 3°C	MAX 19.5°C MIN 3.5°C
Starling 2	Blackbird	Bluetit 2	Blackbird
Greenfinch 2	Collared dove	Starling 2&5	Bluetit 2
Bluetit 2	Starling 2	Blackbird	Great tit 2
Bullfinch 2	Bluetit 2	Collared dove	Dunnock 2
Collared dove	Bullfinch 2	Chaffinch 3	Starling 2
Great tit	Chaffinch 2	Greenfinch 5	Chaffinch 2
Magpie 2	Greenfinch 2	Dunnock 2	Greenfinch 2
Blackbird	Brambling		Collared dove
	Great Tit		

	26th		27th		28th
Bluetit 2		Collared dove 2		Starlings 2	
Robin		Blackbird 2		Collared dove 2	
Blackbird		Bluetit 2		Bluetit 2	
Collared dove 2		Chaffinch		Blackbird	
Dunnock.		Greenfinch		Blackcap.	
		Dunnock 2		Greenfinch 3	
				Dunnock	
(Leeds library)				Great tit 2	

26th — CURRENT 10°C
MAX 25.0°C MIN 2°C
Starling 2
Collared dove
Blackbird
Dunnock 2
Wren
Coal tit
Bluetit 2
Greenfinch 3

27th — CURRENT 14°C
MAX 24.5°C MIN 0.5°C
Blackbird 2
Bluetit 2
Dunnock 2
Starling
Bullfinch (M)
Greenfinch 3

28th — CURRENT 12°C
MAX 25°C MIN 0°C
Blackbird
Dunnock 2
Bullfinch (M&F)
Bluetit 2
Greenfinch
Wren
Starling 2

26th — CURRENT 10.5°C
MAX 21°C MIN 3°C
Starlings 9   Brambling 2
Blackbird 2
Dunnock 2
Bluetit
Bullfinch 2
Collared dove 2
Chaffinch
Greenfinch
Wren

27th — CURRENT 11.5°C
MAX 30°C MIN 0°C
Starling 3
Greenfinch 2
Bluetit
Collared dove
Chaffinch
Bullfinch
Crow
Magpie

28th — CURRENT 6.5°C
MAX 21.5°C MIN 5°C
Bluetit 2   Dunnock 2
Blackbird
Starling 26
Wren
Chaffinch
Greenfinch 5
Collared dove 3
Brambling
Magpie

ADDITIONAL NOTES:
2001. Aggressive bluetits mobbing chaffinch, greenfinch. Nest building on 25 & 27th.
2002 March 24 M & F Bullfinch return
" 26' Wren
2002 28th March bumble bee!

Song thrush nests were once easy to find at this time of the year but sadly this is no longer the case. Song thrush numbers have fallen by a staggering seventy-three per cent over the last twenty-five years. Intensive field studies are now underway and it is hoped that solutions can be found and the decline halted.

Song thrush nest

MARCH

YEAR 1 2001 — 29th	30th	31st	ADDITIONAL NOTES:
Collared Doves 2 Blackbird Bluetit Dunnock Blackcap Greenfinch	2 Bluetits Blackcap Blackbird 2 Collared Doves Dunnock	Bluetits 2 Blackbird 2 Black cap greenfinch wood pigeon coal tit dunnock 2 Collared dove 2	← 1 bumble bee!

YEAR 2 CURRENT 7·5°C — 29th MAX 23·5°C MIN 3·5°C	CURRENT 10°C — 30th MAX 20·5°C MIN 7·5°C	SUN WK 1. CURRENT 12·5°C — 31st MAX 16·5°C MIN 10·5°C
Starling 2 Bluetit 2 Blackbird 2 Dunnock Bullfinch (M+F) Greenfinch	Starling 3 Blackbird 2 Bluetit 2 Magpie 2 Dunnock	Blackbird 2 Bluetit 2 Collared dove Dunnock 2 Starling 2 (Easter)

YEAR 3 CURRENT 12°C — 29th MAX 20°C MIN 3°C	CURRENT 5°C — 30th MAX 21·5°C MIN 1·5°C	CURRENT 7·5°C — 31st MAX 24°C MIN 6·5°C
Blackbird Starling Bluetit 2	Blackbird Greenfinch 2 Dunnock 2 Starling 2 Bluetit 2 Chaffinch 2 Brambling	Bluetit 2 Starling 4 Collared dove 2 Great Tit 2 Bullfinch 2 Greenfinch 3 Magpie 2

MARCH

Many bird species have elaborate courtship displays, one of the most bizarre can be seen this month. Great crested grebes court each other on the water with a 'dance' sequence which contains head shaking, diving and feather fluffing, culminating in a presentation of water weeds whilst rising from the water, breast to breast.

Great crested grebes

APRIL CHECKLIST

YEAR	1	2	3
DIVERS			
Red-throated diver			
Black-throated diver			
Great Northern diver			
GREBES			
Little grebe			
Great crested grebe			
Red-necked grebe			
Slavonian grebe			
Black-necked grebe			
SHEARWATERS			
Fulmar			
Cory's shearwater			
Great shearwater			
Sooty shearwater			
Manx shearwater			
Mediterranean shearwater			
STORM PETRELS			
Storm petrel			
Leach's petrel			
GANNETS			
Gannet			
CORMORANTS			
Cormorant			
Shag			
HERONS			
Bittern			
Night heron			
Little egret			
Great white egret			
Grey heron			
Purple heron			
IBISES			
Spoonbill			
DUCKS			
Mute swan			
Bewick's swan			
Whooper swan			
Bean goose			
Pink-footed goose			
White-fronted goose			
Greylag goose			
Snow goose			
Canada goose			
Barnacle goose			
Brent goose			
Egyptian goose			
Shelduck			
Mandarin			
Wigeon			
American wigeon			
Gadwall			
Teal			
Mallard			
Pintail			
Garganey			
Shoveler			
Red-crested pochard			

YEAR	1	2	3
DUCKS (cont.)			
Pochard			
Ring-necked duck			
Ferruginous duck			
Tufted duck			
Scaup			
Eider			
King eider			
Long-tailed duck			
Common scoter			
Surf scoter			
Velvet scoter			
Goldeneye			
Smew			
Red-breasted merganser			
Goosander			
Ruddy duck			
HAWKS			
Honey buzzard			
Black kite			
Red kite			
White-tailed eagle			
Marsh harrier			
Hen harrier			
Montagu's harrier			
Goshawk			
Sparrowhawk		✓	
Buzzard			
Rough-legged buzzard			
Golden eagle			
OSPREYS			
Osprey			
FALCONS			
Kestrel			
Red-footed falcon			
Merlin			
Hobby			
Peregrine			
GROUSE			
Red grouse			
Ptarmigan			
Black grouse			
Capercaillie			
PHEASANTS			
Red-legged partridge			
Grey partridge			
Quail			
Pheasant			
Golden pheasant			
Lady Amherst's pheasant			
RAILS			
Water rail			
Spotted crake			
Corncrake			
Moorhen			
Coot			
CRANES			
Crane			

YEAR	1	2	3
OYSTERCATCHERS			
Oystercatcher			
AVOCETS			
Black-winged stilt			
Avocet			
THICK-KNEES			
Stone curlew			
PLOVERS			
Little ringed plover			
Ringed plover			
Kentish plover			
Dotterel			
Golden plover			
Grey plover			
Lapwing			
Turnstone			
SANDPIPERS			
Knot			
Sanderling			
Little stint			
Temminck's stint			
White-rumped sandpiper			
Pectoral sandpiper			
Curlew sandpiper			
Purple sandpiper			
Dunlin			
Buff-breasted sandpiper			
Ruff			
Jack snipe			
Snipe			
Woodcock			
Black-tailed godwit			
Bar-tailed godwit			
Whimbrel			
Curlew			
Spotted redshank			
Redshank			
Marsh sandpiper			
Greenshank			
Green sandpiper			
Wood sandpiper			
Common sandpiper			
PHALAROPES			
Red-necked phalarope			
Grey phalarope			
SKUAS			
Pomarine skua			
Arctic skua			
Long-tailed skua			
Great skua			
GULLS			
Mediterranean gull			
Little gull			
Sabine's gull			
Black-headed gull			
Ring-billed gull			
Common gull			
Lesser black-backed gull			

YEAR	1	2	3
GULLS (cont.)			
Herring gull			
Iceland gull			
Glaucous gull			
Great black-backed gull			
Kittiwake			
Sandwich tern			
Roseate tern			
Common tern			
Arctic tern			
Little tern			
Black tern			
White-winged black tern			
AUKS			
Guillemot			
Razorbill			
Black guillemot			
Little auk			
Puffin			
PIGEONS			
Rock dove			
Stock dove			
Wood-pigeon	✓	✓	✓
Collared dove	✓	✓	✓
Turtle dove			
PARROTS			
Ring-necked parakeet			
CUCKOOS			
Cuckoo			
BARN OWLS			
Barn owl			
OWLS			
Snowy owl			
Little owl			
Tawny owl			
Long-eared owl			
Short-eared owl			
NIGHTJARS			
Nightjar			
SWIFTS			
Swift			
Alpine swift			
KINGFISHERS			
Kingfisher			
BEE-EATERS			
Bee-eater			
HOOPOES			
Hoopoe			
WOODPECKERS			
Wryneck			
Green woodpecker			
Great spotted woodpecker.			
Lesser spotted woodpecker.			
LARKS			
Short-toed lark			
Woodlark			
Skylark			
Shore lark			

YEAR	1	2	3
SWALLOWS			
Sand martin			
Swallow			
House martin			
PIPITS			
Richard's pipit			
Tawny pipit			
Tree pipit			
Meadow pipit			
Red-throated pipit			
Rock pipit			
Water pipit			
Yellow wagtail			
Grey wagtail			
Pied wagtail			
WAXWINGS			
Waxwing			
DIPPERS			
Dipper			
WRENS			
Wren		✓	
ACCENTORS			
Dunnock	✓	✓	✓
THRUSHES			
Robin	✓	✓	✓
Nightingale			
Bluethroat			
Black redstart			
Redstart			
Whinchat			
Stonechat			
Wheatear			
Ring ouzel			
Blackbird	✓	✓	✓
Fieldfare			
Song thrush			
Redwing			
Mistle thrush			
FLYCATCHERS			
Cetti's warbler			
Grasshopper warbler			
Savi's warbler			
Aquatic warbler			
Sedge warbler			
Marsh warbler			
Reed warbler			
Icterine warbler			
Melodious warbler			
Dartford warbler			
Subalpine warbler			
Barred warbler			
Lesser whitethroat			
Whitethroat			
Garden warbler			
Blackcap			
Pallas's warbler			
Yellow-browed warbler			
Wood warbler			

YEAR	1	2	3
FLYCATCHERS (*cont.*)			
Chiffchaff			
Willow warbler			
Goldcrest			
Firecrest			
Spotted flycatcher			
Red-breasted flycatcher			
Pied flycatcher			
REEDLINGS			
Bearded tit			
TITMICE			
Long-tailed tit			
Marsh tit			
Willow tit			
Crested tit			
Coal tit	✓	✓	✓
Blue tit	✓	✓	✓
Great tit	✓	✓	✓
NUTHATCHES			
Nuthatch			
CREEPERS			
Treecreeper			
ORIOLES			
Golden oriole			
SHRIKES			
Red-backed shrike			
Great Grey shrike			
Woodchat shrike			
CROWS			
Jay			
Magpie	✓	✓	✓
Chough			
Jackdaw			
Rook			
Carrion crow		✓	✓
Raven			
STARLINGS			
Starling	✓	✓	✓
SPARROWS			
House sparrow		✓	✓
Tree sparrow			
BUNTINGS			
Lapland bunting			
Snow bunting			
Yellowhammer			
Girl bunting			
Ortolan bunting			
Little bunting			
Reed bunting			
Corn bunting			
FINCHES			
Chaffinch	✓	✓	✓
Brambling			✓
Serin			
Greenfinch	✓	✓	✓
Goldfinch		✓	
Siskin		✓	
Linnet			

YEAR	1	2	3
FINCHES (*cont.*)			
Twite			
Redpoll			✓
Arctic redpoll			
Crossbill			
Scottish crossbill			
Scarlet rosefinch			
Bullfinch	✓	✓	✓
Hawfinch			

NON-LISTED SIGHTINGS ⑭ ⑱ ⑰

Probably the best known of all our summer visitors, swallows return to their favourite nest sites this month. Some birds will have arrived from South Africa in March, but by the end of April even the far north of Scotland will be once again enjoying their company.

APRIL

YEAR 1 2001 — 1st	2nd	3rd	4th
Bluetit 2	Bluetit 2	Bluetit 2	Blackbird 2
Blackbird	Blackbird 2	Blackbird 2	Collared doves 2
Starling	Collared Dove 2	Starling	Bluetit
Dunnock	Starling	Dunnock	Chaffinch
Chaffinch		Coal tit	Dunnock 2
Great Tit			
Greenfinch			
Collared Dove 2 -			
	Ann's, Hebden	(Helmsley)	

YEAR 2 CURRENT 12°C — 1st	CURRENT 5°C — 2nd	CURRENT 15°C — 3rd	CURRENT 10°C — 4th
MAX 17.5°C MIN 1°C	MAX 16.5°C MIN 5°C	MAX 23°C MIN 4.5°C	MAX 24.5°C MIN 4.5°C
Blackbird 2	Blackbird 2	Bluetit 2 Collared dove 2	Bluetit 2
Collared dove	Starling 2	Blackbird	Greenfinch
Bluetit 2	Bluetit 2	Starling 2	Starling 2
Starling 2	Collared dove 4	Dunnock	Blackbird 2
Bullfinch (M+F) 2	Bullfinch (M+F) 2	Siskin 2	Dunnock
Dunnock	Greenfinch 3	Woodpigeon	Collared dove 2
	Dunnock	Robin 2	
		Bullfinch 2 (M+F)	
	FOG / MIST		

YEAR 3 CURRENT 8°C — 1st	CURRENT 4°C — 2nd	CURRENT 7.5°C — 3rd	CURRENT 10.5°C — 4th
MAX 12.5°C MIN 2.5°C	MAX 24°C MIN 2.5°C	MAX 22.5°C MIN 7.5°C	MAX 31°C MIN 9°C
Starling 24	Collared dove 23	Greenfinch 3	Red poll *
Greenfinch 85	Starling 3	Dunnock	Starling 5
Dunnock 2	Blackbird	Bullfinch 2	Collared dove 2
Bluetit	Bluetit 3	Bluetit 2	Bluetit 2
Collared dove 2	Greenfinch 23	Chaffinch	Greenfinch
Brambling	Dunnock 2	Blackbird	Brambling 2
Chaffinch 2	Woodpigeon	Collared dove	Dunnock 2
Blackbird 2		Starlings 23	
1st rain for more than 2 weeks			

APRIL

	5th	6th	7th
Blackbird 2		Bluetit 2	Bluetit 2
Chaff mdv		Blackbird 2	Blackbird 2
Bluetit 2		Dunnock 2	Great tit
Robin		Collared dove 2	Dunnock 2
Collared dove 3		Greenfinch 2	Greenfinch
Greenfinch		Wood pigeon	Collared doves 2
dunnock			
			Rugby.

CURRENT 7°C
MAX 20.5°C MIN 4.5°C — 5th
Blackbird 2
Bluetit
Chaffinch
Starling 2
Collared dove 1
Dunnock

CURRENT 6.5°C
MAX 27°C MIN 0.5°C — 6th
Blackbird

Helmsley

CURRENT 2.5°C SUN WK2
MAX 29°C MIN 0.5°C — 7th
Bluetit
Collared dove

Brimham

CURRENT 11°C
MAX 30.5°C MIN 8°C — 5th
Blackbird 2
Dunnock 2
Bluetit 2
Collared dove 2
Bullfinch (M&F) 2
Starling 7
Brambling 3
Greenfinch 24
Great tit 2

CURRENT 9°C
WK 2 Sun
MAX 14°C MIN 3°C — 6th
Starling 6   Chaffinch 3
Collared dove 2   Great tit 2
Blackbird
Greenfinch 23
Bluetit 2
Bullfinch 23 (2M 1F)
Dunnock 2
Brambling
Brimham

CURRENT 9°C
MAX 32.5°C MIN -1°C — 7th
Blackbird 2
Dunnock 2
Bluetit 2
Starling 3
Collared dove 2
Greenfinch
Chaffinch

209
ADDITIONAL NOTES:
4th Collared doves mating on pergola!
2002, Blackbirds nesting in leylandii
" Cat now discovered this nest. Saw
" him at top of leylandii
Robin found mate - feeding her @ b. table!
" Female B. Bird turned up 4.45 pm
2003 4th April Redpoll again on Black S.F.S.

Redstarts begin to arrive this month.
Attractive members of the thrush family
are found throughout England, Wales
and Scotland but only occasionally
breed in Ireland. Both sexes have the
bright russet rump and tail which gives
the bird its name.

Redstart

APRIL

YEAR 1	8th	9th	10th	11th
		2 Blackbirds	Greenfinch	Collared doves 4
		2 Dunnocks	Bluetit 2	Bluetit
		2 Collared doves	Blackbird 2	Blackbird 2
		2 Bluetits	Collared dove 2	
		1 Coaltit	Bullfinch 2 M+F	
		2 Great Tits	Starling	
		Starling	Chaffinch (F)	
				Leeds most of day Library
Rugby.				

YEAR 2 CURRENT 2°C 8th	CURRENT 7°C 9th	CURRENT 7°C 10th	CURRENT 5.5°C 11th
MAX 20.5°C MIN 2.5°C	MAX 20°C MIN 2°C	MAX 25°C MIN 0.5°C	MAX 19°C MIN 3.5°C
Robin 2	Blackbird 2 Magpie	Blackbird 2+ Robin	Bluetit
Blackbird 2	Collared dove 2	Collared dove 2	Starling
Greenfinch	Bluetit	Starling 2	Greenfinch
Dunnock	Woodpigeon	Bluetit 2	Bullfinch (M+F)
Starling 2	Starling 2	Bullfinch (F)	Dunnock
Collared dove	~~Woodpi~~	Greenfinch 2-3	Collared dove 2
Wren	Greenfinch	Goldfinch	Woodpigeon
~~Starling 2~~	Dunnock	Dunnock	
WHITE FROST AM		WHITE FROST AM	

YEAR 3 CURRENT 3.5°C 8th	CURRENT 3°C 9th	CURRENT 4.5°C 10th	CURRENT 2°C 11th
MAX 26.5°C MIN 0°C	MAX 29°C MIN -0.5°C	MAX 29°C MIN -0.5°C	MAX MIN
Bluetit	Blackbird Coal tit	Blackbird 2 Chaffinch	Blackbird 2
Dunnock 2	Starling 2 Robin	Magpie	
Greenfinch 4	Bluetit	Bluetit 2	
Collared dove 3	Collared dove 3	Greenfinch 2	
Brambling 2 (M+F)	Brambling (M+F) 2	Starling 2	
Starling 5	Greenfinch	Collared dove 2+	
Great tit	Chaffinch (F)	Great tit	
Bullfinch (M)	Dunnock	House sparrow 2	
Blackbird	Woodpigeon	Dunnock	Newquay

APRIL

	12th
Collared dove 24	
Blackbird 2	
Greenfinch 2	
Chaffinch	
Starling	
Dunnock 2	
Bluetit 2	

	13th
Bullfinch 2 (M+F)	
Collared Dove 2	
Starling 2	
Dunnock 2	
Blackbird 2	
Greenfinch	

14th

Helmsley / Scarborough

Helmsley / Scarborough

CURRENT 5ºC — 12th
MAX 20.5ºC MIN 1ºC
- Greenfinch 2
- Starling 2
- Woodpigeon
- Blackbird
- Robin
- Collared dove

CURRENT 5.5ºC — 13th
MAX 24ºC MIN 2.5ºC
- Blackbird
- Starling 36
- Collared dove 2
- Bluetit
- Wood pigeon
- Robin
- Greenfinch 2

SUN WK3 CURRENT 8.5ºC — 14th
MAX — MIN 5ºC
- Starling 24
- Bluetit 2
- Chaffinch (M)
- Greenfinch
- Blackbird 2
- Collared dove
- Goldfinch 2 (M&F)
- Robin

12th

Sun Wk 3. — 13th

MAX 27ºC MIN 0ºC — 14th

Newquay

Newquay

Newquay

ADDITIONAL NOTES:
10th 2002. Goldfinch first since July 2001
14th " 2 Goldfinch on birdfeeder!

Not a member of the tit family at all, but the only European representative of the babbler family. The bearded tit is also known as the reedling. These enigmatic little birds are able to alter their digestive systems, feeding on insects all summer and reed seeds throughout the winter months.

Bearded tit

APRIL

YEAR 1 2001 15th	16th	17th	18th
Dunnock 2 Chaffinch Greenfinch 2 Woodpigeon Collared dove 2 Bluetit 2 Starling 2,4 Blackbird 2,3 Coal tit Magpie Bullfinch 2 (M+F)	Bluetit 2 Blackbird 2 Greenfinch 2 Collared dove 2 Starling 2 Dunnock 2 (Overnight frost) Helmsley / Scarborough	Blackbird 3 Wintry Bluetit 2 showers Greenfinch 3 of Great tit 2 snow Collared dove 2 hail Coal Tit 2 Dunnock Starling 2 Chaffinch 2	→

YEAR 2 CURRENT 8°C 15th	CURRENT 7·5°C 16th	CURRENT 4·5°C 17th	CURRENT 10·5°C 18th
MAX 34°C MIN 0·5°C Bluetit Crow Collared dove 2 H Sparrow Starling 2 Robin Greenfinch 2,3 Chaffinch (M) Robin Goldfinch (M+F) Dunnock	MAX 27·5°C MIN 2°C Starling 3 Robin Bluetit 2 Collared dove 2,3 Blackbird Crow Magpie	MAX (NOT CANCELLED FROM 16th) MIN — Blackbird Starling 3,4 Bluetit Goldfinch (F) (M+F) Greenfinch Robin Collared dove 2	MAX 22°C MIN 3·5°C Collared dove Bluetit Starling Scarborough

YEAR 3 CURRENT 12·5°C 15th	CURRENT 14·5°C 16th	CURRENT 12°C 17th	CURRENT 13·5°C 10am 18th
MAX 26°C MIN 7·5°C Collared dove 2 Greenfinch 2,3 Brambling (M) Starling 2 Bluetit Blackbird 2 Great tit 2 Dunnock 2 Woodpigeon	MAX 32·5°C MIN 7·5°C Collared dove 2 Dunnock Starling 2 Bluetit 2 Blackbird 2 Brambling (M) Great tit Temp record for April for hoods set to-day from Met Office.	MAX 27°C MIN 6·5°C Bluetit Greenfinch 2 Starling 7 Collared dove Woodpigeon Magpie	MAX 27°C MIN 4°C Starling 4 Dunnock 2 Bluetit 2 Collared dove 2 Greenfinch 2 Blackbird 2

2001	19th	20th	21st
Bluetit Wintry	Dunnock	Bluetit 2	
Chaffinch Showers	Blackbird 2	Starling 3	
Greenfinch of	Collared dove	Dunnock	
Starlings 5 7 Snow	Great Tit 2	Blackbird	
SPARROWHAWK (m)	Greenfinch	Great Tit 2	
Collared dove 2	Bluetit	Woodpigeon 2	
Blackbird 2	Starlings 4		
Great Tit 2		Overnight frost	
Dunnock Overnight frost	Overnight frost	Helmsley/Malton	

CURRENT 9.5°C 19th	CURRENT 6.30a.m. 4°C 20th	CURRENT — SUN WK4 21st	
MAX 19°C MIN 3.5°C	MAX 27°C? MIN 4°C	MAX 27.5°C MIN 4°C	
Starling	Woodpigeon	Woodpigeon	
Blackbird 2	Starling		
Woodpigeon	Blackbird		
Bluetit	Bluetit		
Chaffinch (M)	Coal tit! V. early morning 7am		
Goldfinch (M)	Great tit 2 " " "		
Collared dove 2			
	London	London	

CURRENT 12°C 19th	SUN.WK4 CURRENT 11°C 20th	CURRENT 9°C 21st	
MAX 18°C MIN 4°C	MAX 24°C MIN 6°C	MAX 26°C MIN 4°C	
Bullfinch (M)	Bluetit 2	Blackbird	
Starling 11	Collared dove	Bluetit	
Bluetit	Starling	Starling 3	
Greenfinch 3		Coal tit	
Great tit			
Blackbird 2			
Dunnock			
Collared dove 2			
Bullfinch (M)	Brimham	Brimham	

ADDITIONAL NOTES:

It is very satisfying to hear of a success story in a world which, at times, seems to be full of ecological doom and gloom. The osprey population is on the increase! In 1959 after an absence of fifty years a pair of ospreys successfully raised young in Scotland. Today, thanks to vigilant protection, some hundred young ospreys leave nests in Scotland every year.

Osprey

APRIL

YEAR 1 2001 22nd	23rd	24th	25th
Bluetit	Blackbird	2 Bluetit	Blackbird 2
Blackbird 2	Bluetit	Blackbird	Bluetit
Starling	Dunnock	Starlings 6	Bullfinch 2 M + F
Wood pigeon	2 Wood pigeons	Greenfinch	Woodpigeon
Coal Tit 2			Greenfinch
Collared dove			
Greenfinch			
Dunnock			
	Leeds am.		Malton

YEAR 2 2002 CURRENT 14°C 22nd	CURRENT 14.5°C 23rd	CURRENT 10.5°C 24th	CURRENT 9.5°C 25th
MAX 27.5°C MIN 4°C	MAX 23°C MIN 9°C	MAX 29.5°C MIN 8.5°C	MAX 29.5°C MIN 8°C
Blackbird	Starling	Great tit 2	Blackbird
Starling	Blackbird 2	Blackbird	Bluetit
	Bluetit	Dunnock.	Starling 2
		Collared dove	Woodpigeon 2
		Starling 2	Coal tit
		Woodpigeon	
		Coal tit	

YEAR 3 2003 CURRENT 8.5°C 22nd	CURRENT 11°C 23rd	CURRENT 10.5°C 24th	CURRENT 10°C 25th
MAX 28°C MIN 2.5°C	MAX 24.5°C MIN 3.5°C	MAX 19.5°C MIN 8°C	MAX 15.5°C MIN 5°C
Bluetit	Collared dove 3	Dunnock	Bluetit
Starling 25	Starling & 56	Bluetit 2	Starlings 45
Greenfinch 2	Bluetit	Greenfinch	Greenfinch
Collared dove 3	H. Sparrow	Starling 2	Bullfinch (M)
Crow	Bullfinch (MF) 2	Great tit	Collared dove 2
Coal tit	Greenfinch &3	Collared dove 2	Blackbird
	Dunnock	Magpie	~~Woodpig~~
			Bullfinch (F)
Mansfield		FA ~ Burnham	Harrogate Flower Show Squirrel

APRIL

2005 27th. Male blackbird feeding
1 fledgling 3x on lawn.
28th feeding fledgling again (Male)

26th	27th	28th
Blackbird 2	Bluetit 2	Greenfinch
Bluetit 2	Blackbird 2	Collared dove
Woodpigeon 2		Blackbird
Greenfinch		Bluetit 2
Collared doves 3		Wood pigeon 2
	Harrogate Spring Flower Show	

26th	27th	28th
CURRENT 9.5°C	CURRENT 4.5°C	SUN. WK.5 CURRENT. 12.5°C
MAX 17°C MIN 3°C	MAX 18°C MIN 4.5°C	MAX 17°C MIN 2.5°C
Woodpigeon	Starling 37	Woodpigeon 2
Starling	Greenfinch 2	Blackbird
Blackbird	Blackbird 2	Starling
	Collared dove	Collared dove
	Bluetit 2	
	Woodpigeon	
RAIN PROPER FOR OVER 3 WKS.		High wind chill factor.

26th	27th	28th
CURRENT (9.50am) 12°C	SUN. WK5 CURRENT 12.5°C 9.15	CURRENT 11.5°C
MAX 30.5°C MIN 7.5°C	MAX 26.5°C MIN 10.5°C	MAX 27.5°C MIN 10°C
Greenfinch	(fledgling) Blackbird x3 Chaffinch (F)	Starling 4
Starling 2	Starling 2+6 Woodpigeon	Woodpigeon
Blackbird 2	Bullfinch 2	Collared dove
Collared dove	Bluetit	Greenfinch
Bullfinch (M.F) 2	Great tit 2	
	Greenfinch 2	
	Coal tit	
	Dunnock	
Leeds Rain 1st for 6 wks or more	Collared dove 2	Torrential rain Sun night mon morning.

Some fifty years or so ago pied flycatchers only bred in Wales, but today they
can be found in the south-west, upland
England and parts of Scotland. They are
natural hole nesters and it is thought
that the provision of nest boxes has
helped them extend their breeding
range.

Pied flycatcher

APRIL

YEAR 1 2001 29th	30th
Blackbird	Blackbirds 23
Starling 23	Bluetit 2
Coal tit	Greenfinch
Greenfinch 24	Starlings 2
Bluetit 2	Woodpigeon
Collared dove	
Dunnock	

YEAR 2 CURRENT 6·5°C 29th MAX 20·5°C MIN 4·5°C	CURRENT 8·5°C 30th MAX 25°C MIN 5·5°C
Blackbird 2	Blackbird 2
Starling 2	Bluetit 2
Great tit 1	Greenfinch
Bluetit	Magpie
Crow	Starling 4
Chaffinch (M)	
Greenfinch	

YEAR 3 CURRENT 12°C 29th MAX 21°C MIN 9°C	CURRENT 13·0C 30th MAX 26°C MIN 7°C
Blackbird 2 (fledgling)	Blackbird 2
Bullfinch (M)	Chaffinch
Woodpigeon	Starling 5
	Collared dove 2
	Bluetit
	Woodpigeon
	Greenfinch
York.	Bullfinch (F M) 2

APRIL

Back from Africa this month comes a bird whose presence, to many people, announces the start of summer. The male cuckoo has one of the best known calls of all our summer visitors, it must be one of the only birds whose voice is more familiar than its appearance.

Cuckoo

MAY CHECKLIST

YEAR	1	2	3
DIVERS			
Red-throated diver			
Black-throated diver			
Great Northern diver			
GREBES			
Little grebe			
Great crested grebe			
Red-necked grebe			
Slavonian grebe			
Black-necked grebe			
SHEARWATERS			
Fulmar			
Cory's shearwater			
Great shearwater			
Sooty shearwater			
Manx shearwater			
Mediterranean shearwater			
STORM PETRELS			
Storm petrel			
Leach's petrel			
GANNETS			
Gannet			
CORMORANTS			
Cormorant			
Shag			
HERONS			
Bittern			
Night heron			
Little egret			
Great white egret			
Grey heron			
Purple heron			
IBISES			
Spoonbill			
DUCKS			
Mute swan			
Bewick's swan			
Whooper swan			
Bean goose			
Pink-footed goose			
White-fronted goose			
Greylag goose			
Snow goose			
Canada goose			
Barnacle goose			
Brent goose			
Egyptian goose			
Shelduck			
Mandarin			
Wigeon			
American wigeon			
Gadwall			
Teal			
Mallard			
Pintail			
Garganey			
Shoveler			
Red-crested pochard			

YEAR	1	2	3
DUCKS (cont.)			
Pochard			
Ring-necked duck			
Ferruginous duck			
Tufted duck			
Scaup			
Eider			
King eider			
Long-tailed duck			
Common scoter			
Surf scoter			
Velvet scoter			
Goldeneye			
Smew			
Red-breasted merganser			
Goosander			
Ruddy duck			
HAWKS			
Honey buzzard			
Black kite			
Red kite			
White-tailed eagle			
Marsh harrier			
Hen harrier			
Montagu's harrier			
Goshawk			
Sparrowhawk			
Buzzard			
Rough-legged buzzard			
Golden eagle			
OSPREYS			
Osprey			
FALCONS			
Kestrel			
Red-footed falcon			
Merlin			
Hobby			
Peregrine			
GROUSE			
Red grouse			
Ptarmigan			
Black grouse			
Capercaillie			
PHEASANTS			
Red-legged partridge			
Grey partridge			
Quail			
Pheasant			
Golden pheasant			
Lady Amherst's pheasant			
RAILS			
Water rail			
Spotted crake			
Corncrake			
Moorhen			
Coot			
CRANES			
Crane			

YEAR	1	2	3
OYSTERCATCHERS			
Oystercatcher			
AVOCETS			
Black-winged stilt			
Avocet			
THICK-KNEES			
Stone curlew			
PLOVERS			
Little ringed plover			
Ringed plover			
Kentish plover			
Dotterel			
Golden plover			
Grey plover			
Lapwing			
Turnstone			
SANDPIPERS			
Knot			
Sanderling			
Little stint			
Temminck's stint			
White-rumped sandpiper			
Pectoral sandpiper			
Curlew sandpiper			
Purple sandpiper			
Dunlin			
Buff-breasted sandpiper			
Ruff			
Jack snipe			
Snipe			
Woodcock			
Black-tailed godwit			
Bar-tailed godwit			
Whimbrel			
Curlew			
Spotted redshank			
Redshank			
Marsh sandpiper			
Greenshank			
Green sandpiper			
Wood sandpiper			
Common sandpiper			
PHALAROPES			
Red-necked phalarope			
Grey phalarope			
SKUAS			
Pomarine skua			
Arctic skua			
Long-tailed skua			
Great skua			
GULLS			
Mediterranean gull			
Little gull			
Sabine's gull			
Black-headed gull			
Ring-billed gull			
Common gull			
Lesser black-backed gull			

YEAR	1	2	3
GULLS (cont.)			
Herring gull			
Iceland gull			
Glaucous gull			
Great black-backed gull			
Kittiwake			
Sandwich tern			
Roseate tern			
Common tern			
Arctic tern			
Little tern			
Black tern			
White-winged black tern			
AUKS			
Guillemot			
Razorbill			
Black guillemot			
Little auk			
Puffin			
PIGEONS			
Rock dove			
Stock dove			
Wood-pigeon	✓	✓	✓
Collared dove	✓	✓	✓
Turtle dove			
PARROTS			
Ring-necked parakeet			
CUCKOOS			
Cuckoo			
BARN OWLS			
Barn owl			
OWLS			
Snowy owl			
Little owl			
Tawny owl			
Long-eared owl			
Short-eared owl			
NIGHTJARS			
Nightjar			
SWIFTS			
Swift			
Alpine swift			
KINGFISHERS			
Kingfisher			
BEE-EATERS			
Bee-eater			
HOOPOES			
Hoopoe			
WOODPECKERS			
Wryneck			
Green woodpecker			
Great spotted woodpecker.			
Lesser spotted woodpecker			
LARKS			
Short-toed lark			
Woodlark			
Skylark			
Shore lark			

YEAR	1	2	3
SWALLOWS			
Sand martin			
Swallow			
House martin			
PIPITS			
Richard's pipit			
Tawny pipit			
Tree pipit			
Meadow pipit			
Red-throated pipit			
Rock pipit			
Water pipit			
Yellow wagtail			
Grey wagtail			
Pied wagtail			
WAXWINGS			
Waxwing			
DIPPERS			
Dipper			
WRENS			
Wren		✓	✓
ACCENTORS			
Dunnock	✓	✓	✓
THRUSHES			
Robin		✓	
Nightingale			
Bluethroat			
Black redstart			
Redstart			
Whinchat			
Stonechat			
Wheatear			
Ring ouzel			
Blackbird	✓	✓	✓
Fieldfare			
Song thrush			
Redwing			
Mistle thrush			
FLYCATCHERS			
Cetti's warbler			
Grasshopper warbler			
Savi's warbler			
Aquatic warbler			
Sedge warbler			
Marsh warbler			
Reed warbler			
Icterine warbler			
Melodious warbler			
Dartford warbler			
Subalpine warbler			
Barred warbler			
Lesser whitethroat			
Whitethroat			
Garden warbler			
Blackcap			
Pallas's warbler			
Yellow-browed warbler			
Wood warbler			

FLYCATCHERS (cont.)	1	2	3
Chiffchaff			
Willow warbler			
Goldcrest			
Firecrest			
Spotted flycatcher			
Red-breasted flycatcher			
Pied flycatcher			
REEDLINGS			
Bearded tit			
TITMICE			
Long-tailed tit			
Marsh tit			
Willow tit			
Crested tit			
Coal tit	✓	✓	✓
Blue tit	✓	✓	✓
Great tit	✓	✓	✓
NUTHATCHES			
Nuthatch			
CREEPERS			
Treecreeper			
ORIOLES			
Golden oriole			
SHRIKES			
Red-backed shrike			
Great Grey shrike			
Woodchat shrike			
CROWS			
Jay			
Magpie	✓	✓	✓
Chough			
Jackdaw			
Rook	✓		
Carrion crow	✓	✓	✓
Raven			
STARLINGS			
Starling	✓	✓	✓
SPARROWS			
House sparrow			
Tree sparrow			
BUNTINGS			
Lapland bunting			
Snow bunting			
Yellowhammer			
Cirl bunting			
Ortolan bunting			
Little bunting			
Reed bunting			
Corn bunting			
FINCHES			
Chaffinch	✓	✓	✓
Brambling			
Serin			
Greenfinch	✓	✓	✓
Goldfinch		✓	
Siskin			
Linnet			

FINCHES (cont.)	1	2	3
Twite			
Redpoll			
Arctic redpoll			
Crossbill			
Scottish crossbill			
Scarlet rosefinch			
Bullfinch	✓	✓	✓
Hawfinch			

NON-LISTED SIGHTINGS

Spotted flycatchers arrive in May, later than most other summer migrants. They may lack colour but they have a lot of character, sitting bolt upright on their favoured perch with wings and tail flickering, watching for insects.

MAY

YEAR 1 2001 1st	2nd	3rd	4th
Starling 2	Bluetit	Bluetit 2	Blackbird 2
Blackbird	Blackbird 2	Blackbird 2	Collared dove
Great Tit	Collared dove 2	Starling 3	greenfinch
Greenfinch	Wood pigeon	Dunnock	coaltit 2
Collared dove	Magpie	Collared Dove 2	bluetit
	Jackdaw!	Coal Tit 2	
		Woodpigeon	
			Holland
	Helmsley / Malton		

YEAR 2 CURRENT 7.5°C 1st MAX 20°C MIN 3.5°C	CURRENT 8°C 2nd MAX 19°C MIN 3.5°C	CURRENT 10°C 3rd MAX 22°C MIN 3°C	CURRENT 8°C 4th MAX 19.5°C MIN 3.5°C
Starling 5	Woodpigeon	Woodpigeon	Woodpigeon
Blackbird 2	Starling 7	Blackbird (F)(M)(FM)	Bluetit 2
Greenfinch 2	Blackbird	Starling 4	Starling 4
Woodpigeon	Collared dove	Chaffinch (M)	Greenfinch 2
Bluetit 2	Goldfinch	Bluetit	Blackbird (M)
	Chaffinch	Collared dove	

YEAR 3 CURRENT 13°C 1st MAX 20.5°C MIN 7.5°C	CURRENT 12.5°C 2nd MAX 14.5°C MIN 6°C	CURRENT 9.5°C 3rd MAX 19.5°C MIN 9.5°C	SUN. WK 6 CURRENT 13°C 4th MAX 32°C MIN 11°C
Greenfinch	Collared dove 2	Blackbird	Greenfinch
Starling 4	Starling 3	Starling 3	Bullfinch (M)
Collared dove	Great tit	Greenfinch	Starling 2
Blackbird	Bullfinch	Bluetit 2	Woodpigeon 2
	Coco	Collared dove 3	
	Magpie		
			Brimham

MAY

	5th		6th		7th
				Wood pigeon 2	
				Bullfinch M	
				Collared dove 2	
				Dunnock	
				Blackbird	
				Crow	
Holland		Holland		Holland.	

5th CURRENT 8°C WK 6 SUD
MAX 25.5°C MIN 6.5°C
Blackbird 3
Starling 26
Collared dove
Chaffinch 2 (M+F)
Woodpigeon

6th CURRENT 7.5°C
MAX 22.5°C MIN 7.5°C
Blackbird
Chaffinch
Woodpigeon
Starling 8

7th CURRENT 10°C
MAX 17°C MIN 9°C
Starling 8   Chaffinch (M)
Woodpigeon
Blackbird (M)
Great tit
Coal tit
Goldfinch (2
Bluetit
Collared dove

5th Strong NE wind High Chill factor
CURRENT 14°C (9.30)
MAX 32°C MIN 8°C
Blackbird (M+F)
Starling 3
Collared dove 23
Bluetit 2

6th Overcast, misty, strong wind
CURRENT 11.5°C (9.30)
MAX 27.5°C MIN 8°C
Starling 2+3
Blackbird (M)
Woodpigeon
Greenfinch

7th CURRENT 12.5°C
MAX   MIN
Starling 35
Bluetit
Collared dove
Greenfinch 3
Blackbird (M+F) 2

HULL — KELKENOF

ADDITIONAL NOTES: Yr 1.
2 Coal tits 3rd May, backwards
& forwards most of day, presumably
feeding young
3rd May Baby Blackbird, quite few
feathers inc. wing found dead on pathway
beneath wisteria Nick in throat magpie?
6th Saw crow in hedge where b'birds nest is

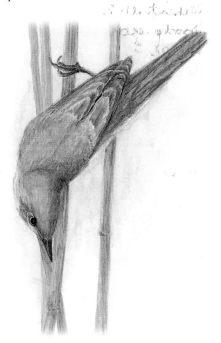

Reed warblers are mostly found in the
south-east of England. As their name
suggests, they favour reed beds, returning from Africa in late spring, when the
new reed growth is at the right height to
provide suitable nest sites.

Reed warbler

MAY

YEAR 1 2001 8th	9th	10th	11th
Starlings 35	Blackbird 2	Blackbirds 2	Starling
Blackbird	Bluetit	Greenfinch 2	Blackbird
Chaffinch	Starling 24	Starling 2	Greenfinch
Bullfinch M & F	Bullfinch M & F		Dunnock
Greenfinch 2	Greenfinch 2		Bluetit
Bluetit	Collared dove 1		Coal Tit
Collared dove 2	Dunnock		
Coal Tit	Chaffinch		

YEAR 2 CURRENT 12°C 8th	CURRENT 11°C 9th	CURRENT 12°C 10th	CURRENT 10°C 11th
MAX 18°C MIN 6.5°C	MAX 16.5°C MIN 7.5°C	MAX 22.5°C MIN 9.5°C	
Blackbird (M)	Blackbird jny robin	Collared dove 2 Magpie	Starling 5
Starling 3 11	Starling 36 12 Chaffinch (F)	Starling 3 Goldfinch (2 M&F)	Woodpigeon
Chaffinch 2 (M&F)	Greenfinch	Bluetit 2	Bluetit
Woodpigeon	Bullfinch (F)	Coal tit	Bullfinch (M)
Magpie	Woodpigeon	Woodpigeon 2	
Collared dove	Bluetit	Crow	
	Great tit	Greenfinch	
	Magpie	Blackbird	
		Great tit	RUGBY

YEAR 3 8th	CURRENT 15°C (11am) 9th	CURRENT 13°C 10th	SUNNK. 70 11th
MAX 32°C MIN 6°C	MAX 26°C MIN 4.5°C	MAX MIN	MAX 30.5° MIN 5°C
	Collared dove 24	Greenfinch	
	Bluetit	Starling 4	
	Dunnock 2	Magpie	
	Blackbird 2	Crow	
	Starling 2		
	Greenfinch		
KEUKENHOF	KEUKENHOF / HULL	JACKIE'S RUGBY	RUGBY

MAY

2002 8th Hand connection, out in
time to see magpie fly off with baby
blackbird in its beak.

ADDITIONAL NOTES:
2002 16th Bluetits hatched over w/end.

Lapwings started their breeding season back in March, and by May many will have youngsters to care for. Their simple nest is usually sited in an exposed area, typically in a ploughed field. Soon after hatching, the parent birds lead the young away from the nest to nearby cover.

	12th		13th		14th
Woodpigeon		Starling 27		Starling 5	
Blackbird		Greenfinch		Blackbird 1	
Starling		Dunnock		Collared dove	
Coal tit		Blackbird 2		Bullfinch (M)	
Greenfinch 2		Bullfinch (M)		Greenfinch 3	
Collared dove		Coal tit		Bluetit 2	
Dunnock		Bluetit		Coal Tit	
Chaffinch		Collared Dove			
		Woodpigeon			

SUN. WR7. 12th	CURRENT 12.5°C 13th	CURRENT 15°C 14th
MAX 24.5°C MIN 5.5°C	MAX 15.5°C MIN 10°C	MAX 25.5°C MIN 9.5°C
	Starling 4	Starling 5
	Blackbird	Bluetit 2
	Bluetit 3	Chaffinch (F)
	Dunnock Robin	Blackbird
	Bullfinch (M)	Goldfinch
		Magpie
		Great tit

RUGBY

CURRENT 10°C 12th	CURRENT 8.5°C 13th	CURRENT 10°C 14th
MAX 26°C MIN 4.5°C	MAX 19.5°C MIN 5.5°C	MAX 20.5°C MIN 4°C
Great tit	Blackbird 2	Starling 2 5
Starling 4 5	Starling 4 5 11	Wren
Blackbird (F)	Bluetit	Bluetit
Dunnock 2	Dunnock 2	Dunnock
Bluetit	Greenfinch	Crow
Collared dove 2	Crow	Woodpigeon
	Collared dove	
	Chaffinch	
	Woodpigeon	Mouse

Lapwing

MAY

YEAR 1 2001 · 15th	16th	17th	18th
Starlings 2	Coal tit	Bullfinch (M) & (F)	Collared dove
Blackbird 2	Collared dove	Coal Tit	Starling
Bluetit 2	Blackbird	Greenfinch	Coal tit 2
Greenfinch 2	Starling	Bluetit	Bullfinch (M)
Crow	Bluetit 2	Starling 5	Chaffinch (F)
Chaffinch (M)	Dunnock 2	Blackbird	Dunnock
Bullfinch (M)		Collared dove 3	
Collared dove		Robin !! Hurray! *	
		Dunnock	

YEAR 2 CURRENT 14°C · 15th MAX 29°C MIN 9°C	CURRENT 9°C · 16th MAX 38°C MIN 9°C	CURRENT 20°C · 17th MAX 58°C MIN 8·5°C	CURRENT 10°C · 18th MAX 19°C MIN 10°C
Starling 8	Blackbird	Bluetit	Blackbird 2
Woodpigeon	Starling 2	Blackbird	Starling 23
Blackbird	Woodpigeon	Starling 4	Bluetit 2
Greenfinch	Bluetit 2	Collared dove	Woodpigeon
Dunnock		Magpie	Goldfinch 2 (M&F)
Bluetit		Woodpigeon	
Chaffinch (M)			
Collared dove 2			
Showery - cloudy			Wet / damp / misty

YEAR 3 CURRENT 9°C · 15th MAX 28°C MIN 7°C	CURRENT 12·5°C (9.50) · 16th MAX 17·5°C MIN 10°C	CURRENT 16°C (9.30) · 17th MAX 22·5°C MIN 10·5°C	SUN LWB CURRENT 15·5°C · 18th MAX 28°C MIN 7·5°C
Dunnock 2	Chaffinch (M)	Blackbird 2 Magpie	Starling 8 Bullfinch 2
Blackbird ·	Blackbird 2	Starling 24	Blackbird 2
Starling 9	Starling 2	Greenfinch 2	Collared dove 24
Greenfinch	Collared dove 2	Collared dove 2	Dunnock
Bluetit	Dunnock	Great tit	Coal tit
Collared dove	Bluetit	Dunnock 2	Greenfinch
Great tit White butterfly	Greenfinch 3	Bullfinch 2	Great tit
Coal tit	Woodpigeon 2	Bluetit 2	Woodpigeon
		Woodpigeon	Bluetit

MAY

	19th	SUNDAY	20th		21st
Coal tit		Greenfinch		Bluetit	
Starling 2		Coal tit		Coal tit	
Bullfinch (M) (came twice) am + pm				Starling 3	
Bluetit				Blackbird	
Chaffinch (M)				Magpie	
Dunnock				Dunnock	
Blackbird				Wood pigeon	
Wood pigeon 2					

CURRENT 15.5°C SUN YES 19th	CURRENT 14°C 20th	CURRENT 15°C 21st
MAX 23.5°C MIN 12°C	MAX 19.5°C MIN 12°C	MAX 23°C MIN 11°C
Blackbird	Blackbird 2	Woodpigeon
Bluetit	Bluetit	Bluetit 2
Starling 2	Collared dove 2	Blackbird (F/M) 2
Woodpigeon	Woodpigeon	Collared dove 2
		Starling
		Dunnock
		Greenfinch

sunny periods - cloud

CURRENT 14°C 19th	CURRENT 11.5°C 20th	CURRENT 13°C 21st
MAX 22.5°C MIN 6.5°C	MAX 22.5°C MIN 8.5°C	MAX 18°C MIN 11.5°C
Blackbird	Blackbird 2 3 Robin (Hurray!) *	Blackbird 2 Crow
Dunnock	Bluetit 2	Bluetit
Starling 3 4	Starling 2 3 6	Starling 2 4 5 8
Bluetit	Bullfinch (M)	Dunnock
Greenfinch 2	Greenfinch 3	Woodpigeon
Coal tit	Dunnock	Great tit
Great tit	Great tit	Collared dove
Collared dove 2	Woodpigeon 3	Coal tit
	Collared dove 2	Greenfinch 2

ADDITIONAL NOTES:
14th May Think I heard bluetit nestlings in nesting box for first time.
20th May Coal tit definitely feeding young. Think mistaken by bluetits. Nest may even be deserted, Young starling on lawn.
2003 16th May Saw bluetit with beak full of grubs, then went away across the back. Suspect nest box been deserted as haven't seen bluetits going in or out for nearly 2 wks.
20th May Magpie robbed Blackbird's nest in leylandii. Had fledglings in
21st Mother starling feeding 2 fledglings

Unlike the grey and the pied wagtails, the yellow wagtail is a non resident bird, arriving in Britain in the spring. They are very timid birds and can be difficult to watch at close range. Look for them near rivers, in cattle pastures and water meadows.

Yellow wagtail

MAY

YEAR 1 2001 22nd	23rd	24th	25th
Bluetit	Collared dove 2	Starling 4	Coal tit
Greenfinch	Coal tit	Collared dove	Bluetit 2
Starling 23	dunnock	Bluetit 2	Starling
Coal tit	Blackbird	Blackbird	Blackbird
Blackbird	Bluetit		Dunnock
(Hot & sunny)	(Hot & sunny)	(Hot & Sunny)	

YEAR 2 CURRENT 15.5°C 22nd MAX 29.5°C MIN 11.5°C	CURRENT 17.5°C 23rd MAX 29.5°C MIN 10.5°C	CURRENT 12.5°C 24th MAX 25.5°C MIN 10°C	CURRENT 12.5°C 25th MAX 26.5°C MIN 9.5°C
Blackbird	Blackbird	Blackbird	Blackbird
Starling 25	Woodpigeon 2	Bluetit	Goldfinch (1MF) 2
Dunnock	Greenfinch	Woodpigeon	Bluetit
Woodpigeon	Starling 2	Collared dove	Collared dove 2
	Bluetit 2		Starling
	Dunnock		Dunnock
	Collared dove		Magpie
	Magpie	GALE FORCE WINDS/SHOWERS	

YEAR 3 CURRENT 17°C 22nd MAX 18.5°C MIN 11°C	CURRENT 14°C 23rd MAX 32°C MIN 9.5°C	CURRENT 15.5°C 24th MAX 23°C MIN 8°C	SUN WK 9 CURRENT 18°C 25th MAX 28°C MIN 6.5°C
Woodpigeon 2 Coal tit	Blackbird	Starling 2 Coal tit	Blackbird
Collared dove 2 Magpie	Dunnock 2	Great tit	Collared dove 2
Starling 24	Collared dove	Dunnock 2	Great tit
Great tit	Starling 4	Bullfinch 3!! (2MF)	Robin
Blue tit	Woodpigeon	Bluetit	Starling 23
Dunnock 2	Greenfinch	Greenfinch 2	Dunnock 3
Greenfinch 2		Collared dove 2 4	Greenfinch
Blackbird 2		Blackbird	Bluetit Squirrel
Chaffinch (M)		Magpie 2	

MAY

26th

Blue tit   Dunnock 2
Blackbird 2   Bullfinch (M)
Collared dove 2
Coal tit
Starling
Wood pigeon 2
Greenfinch
Great tit
Chaffinch (M) & (F)

ON. WKG. CURRENT 12°C
MAX 19.5°C MIN 8°C
Starling 8   Collared dove 2
Blue tit 2   Chaffinch (M)
Blackbird   Great tit.
Bullfinch (MF) 2   Woodpigeon
Dunnock 2
Greenfinch
Goldfinch (MF) 2
Coal tit
Heavy showers.

CURRENT 12°C
MAX 30.5°C MIN 11.5°C
Blackbird
Blue tit
Collared dove 2
Dunnock 3
Robin
Bullfinch 2
Greenfinch

27th

SUNDAY
Blackbird 2
Blue tit
Coal tit
Starling
Dunnock
Collared dove

CURRENT 12.5°C
MAX 29°C   MIN 8°C
Blackbird
Blue tit 8
Starling 4
Great tit
Collared dove
Dunnock
Woodpigeon
Coal tit

CURRENT 20.5°C
MAX 26.5°C MIN 13°C
Blackbird
Starling 2
Bullfinch (MF) 2
Greenfinch 2
Blue tit 2
Collared dove 2

28th

Dunnock
Blackbird 2
Coal tit
Bullfinch 2 (M & F)
Blue tit
Starling 2
Collared dove 3
Chaffinch

CURRENT 15.5°C
MAX 19°C? MIN 9.5°C
Blue tit 2   Great tit
Magpie   Dunnock
Greenfinch
Chaffinch (M)
Starling 3
Coal tit
Blackbird
Woodpigeon
Sunny am. Rain pm

CURRENT 19°C
MAX 40°C MIN 13°C
Coal tit
Robin
Greenfinch 2
Starling 45
Blackbird
Collared dove 2

ADDITIONAL NOTES:

ADDITIONAL NOTES:

24th May Saw bluetits feeding offspring in nesting box.
26th May Wet day, swallows or swifts flying low after insects.
27th May 8 young bluetits in Rowan Tree but not from my nesting box.
2003 3 Bullfinches (2 M F) fledgling?

Over the past twenty years the hobby has dramatically increased in numbers, expanding its breeding range northwards and westwards. Having overwintered in Africa these elegant, agile falcons return to Britain in May. Spectacular aerial hunters, they prey on birds and larger insects, including dragonflies.

Hobby

MAY

YEAR 1 2001 29th	30th	31st
Bluetit	Bullfinch	Greenfinch
Starling 2	Starling 5 (F + 4 young)	Blackbird
Blackbird 2	Collared dove	Dunnock
Coal tit	Coal tit	Bluetit 2
Collared dove 2	Blackbird	Collared dove
	Greenfinch	Bullfinch
	Dunnock 2	Coal tit
	Bluetit	Wood pigeon 2
(Out most of day)		

YEAR 2 CURRENT 13°C 29th	CURRENT 12·5°C 30th	CURRENT 12°C 31st
MAX 19°C?? MIN 9·5°C	MAX 30·5°C MIN 8·5°C	MAX 30·5°C MIN 8·5°C
Blackbird	Starling 9	Magpie
Bluetit	Bluetit 2	Great tit
Dunnock	Collared dove	Starling 2
Starling 4	Blackbird	Greenfinch 2
Collared dove	Greenfinch 2	Bluetit 4
Greenfinch 2	Chaffinch (F)	Dunnock
Great tit.		Collared dove 2
		Woodpigeon 2
	FA a Helmsley a Tong.	

My bluetits flew nest
Chased off magpie!

YEAR 3 CURRENT 22°C 29th	CURRENT 25°C 30th	CURRENT 12·5°C (7.30am) 31st
MAX 30·5°C MIN 12°C	MAX 39°C MIN 10·5°C	MAX 38·5°C MIN 12·5°C
Starling 5	Great tit	Starling
Greenfinch	Collared dove	
Coal tit	Starling	
Collared dove	Greenfinch 2	
	Bullfinch (M)	
	Blackbird	
	Coal tit	
		Holker Hall

MAY

Fine weather at this time of the year over western Europe occasionally causes migrating hoopoes to overshoot their normal breeding range and land in Britain. These exotic-looking birds are truly unmistakable and sometimes breed here, mostly in southern and eastern England.

Hoopoe

JUNE CHECKLIST

YEAR	1	2	3
DIVERS			
Red-throated diver			
Black-throated diver			
Great Northern diver			
GREBES			
Little grebe			
Great crested grebe			
Red-necked grebe			
Slavonian grebe			
Black-necked grebe			
SHEARWATERS			
Fulmar			
Cory's shearwater			
Great shearwater			
Sooty shearwater			
Manx shearwater			
Mediterranean shearwater			
STORM PETRELS			
Storm petrel			
Leach's petrel			
GANNETS			
Gannet			
CORMORANTS			
Cormorant			
Shag			
HERONS			
Bittern			
Night heron			
Little egret			
Great white egret			
Grey heron			
Purple heron			
IBISES			
Spoonbill			
DUCKS			
Mute swan			
Bewick's swan			
Whooper swan			
Bean goose			
Pink-footed goose			
White-fronted goose			
Greylag goose			
Snow goose			
Canada goose			
Barnacle goose			
Brent goose			
Egyptian goose			
Shelduck			
Mandarin			
Wigeon			
American wigeon			
Gadwall			
Teal			
Mallard			
Pintail			
Garganey			
Shoveler			
Red-crested pochard			

YEAR	1	2	3
DUCKS (*cont.*)			
Pochard			
Ring-necked duck			
Ferruginous duck			
Tufted duck			
Scaup			
Eider			
King eider			
Long-tailed duck			
Common scoter			
Surf scoter			
Velvet scoter			
Goldeneye			
Smew			
Red-breasted merganser			
Goosander			
Ruddy duck			
HAWKS			
Honey buzzard			
Black kite			
Red kite			
White-tailed eagle			
Marsh harrier			
Hen harrier			
Montagu's harrier			
Goshawk			
Sparrowhawk			
Buzzard			
Rough-legged buzzard			
Golden eagle			
OSPREYS			
Osprey			
FALCONS			
Kestrel			
Red-footed falcon			
Merlin			
Hobby			
Peregrine			
GROUSE			
Red grouse			
Ptarmigan			
Black grouse			
Capercaillie			
PHEASANTS			
Red-legged partridge			
Grey partridge			
Quail			
Pheasant			
Golden pheasant			
Lady Amherst's pheasant			
RAILS			
Water rail			
Spotted crake			
Corncrake			
Moorhen			
Coot			
CRANES			
Crane			

YEAR	1	2	3
OYSTERCATCHERS			
Oystercatcher			
AVOCETS			
Black-winged stilt			
Avocet			
THICK-KNEES			
Stone curlew			
PLOVERS			
Little ringed plover			
Ringed plover			
Kentish plover			
Dotterel			
Golden plover			
Grey plover			
Lapwing			
Turnstone			
SANDPIPERS			
Knot			
Sanderling			
Little stint			
Temminck's stint			
White-rumped sandpiper			
Pectoral sandpiper			
Curlew sandpiper			
Purple sandpiper			
Dunlin			
Buff-breasted sandpiper			
Ruff			
Jack snipe			
Snipe			
Woodcock			
Black-tailed godwit			
Bar-tailed godwit			
Whimbrel			
Curlew			
Spotted redshank			
Redshank			
Marsh sandpiper			
Greenshank			
Green sandpiper			
Wood sandpiper			
Common sandpiper			
PHALAROPES			
Red-necked phalarope			
Grey phalarope			
SKUAS			
Pomarine skua			
Arctic skua			
Long-tailed skua			
Great skua			
GULLS			
Mediterranean gull			
Little gull			
Sabine's gull			
Black-headed gull			
Ring-billed gull			
Common gull			
Lesser black-backed gull			

YEAR	1	2	3
GULLS (*cont.*)			
Herring gull			
Iceland gull			
Glaucous gull			
Great black-backed gull			
Kittiwake			
Sandwich tern			
Roseate tern			
Common tern			
Arctic tern			
Little tern			
Black tern			
White-winged black tern			
AUKS			
Guillemot			
Razorbill			
Black guillemot			
Little auk			
Puffin			
PIGEONS			
Rock dove			
Stock dove			
Wood-pigeon	✓	✓	✓
Collared dove	✓	✓	✓
Turtle dove			
PARROTS			
Ring-necked parakeet			
CUCKOOS			
Cuckoo			
BARN OWLS			
Barn owl			
OWLS			
Snowy owl			
Little owl			
Tawny owl			
Long-eared owl			
Short-eared owl			
NIGHTJARS			
Nightjar			
SWIFTS			
Swift			
Alpine swift			
KINGFISHERS			
Kingfisher			
BEE-EATERS			
Bee-eater			
HOOPOES			
Hoopoe			
WOODPECKERS			
Wryneck			
Green woodpecker			
Great spotted woodpecker			
Lesser spotted woodpecker			
LARKS			
Short-toed lark			
Woodlark			
Skylark			
Shore lark			

YEAR	1	2
SWALLOWS		
Sand martin		
Swallow		
House martin		
PIPITS		
Richard's pipit		
Tawny pipit		
Tree pipit		
Meadow pipit		
Red-throated pipit		
Rock pipit		
Water pipit		
Yellow wagtail		
Grey wagtail		
Pied wagtail		
WAXWINGS		
Waxwing		
DIPPERS		
Dipper		
WRENS		
Wren		✓
ACCENTORS		
Dunnock	✓	✓
THRUSHES		
Robin	✓	✓
Nightingale		
Bluethroat		
Black redstart		
Redstart		
Whinchat		
Stonechat		
Wheatear		
Ring ouzel		
Blackbird	✓	✓
Fieldfare		
Song thrush		
Redwing		
Mistle thrush		
FLYCATCHERS		
Cetti's warbler		
Grasshopper warbler		
Savi's warbler		
Aquatic warbler		
Sedge warbler		
Marsh warbler		
Reed warbler		
Icterine warbler		
Melodious warbler		
Dartford warbler		
Subalpine warbler		
Barred warbler		
Lesser whitethroat		
Whitethroat		
Garden warbler		
Blackcap		
Pallas's warbler		
Yellow-browed warbler		
Wood warbler		

NON-LISTED SIGHTINGS

The puffin's colourful beak is especially adapted to hold small fish. Neatly arranged, they can carry as many as ten at a time back to the nest burrow, to feed their single chick. Once they have fledged, young puffins leave the nest under the cover of darkness to avoid predation from hungry gulls.

JUNE

YEAR 1 2001 1st	2nd	WK.9/10 3rd	4th
Dunnock			
Greenfinch	Blackbird	Blackbird 2	Blackbird
Bluetit	Starling 2.7	Bluetit 3	Woodpigeon 2
Starling 2.7	Bluetit	Greenfinch	Chaffinch
Bullfinch M & F	dunnock	Starling 36	Greenfinch
Collared dove 2	Greenfinch	Chaffinch (F)	Collared dove
Blackbird	Coal tit	Dunnock	Bluetit
	Collared dove	Bullfinch (M & F)	Starling 3
		Woodpigeon 2	
		Collared dove 3	

YEAR 2 CURRENT 16.5°C 1st	SUN WK10 CURRENT 20°C 2nd	CURRENT 19°C 3rd	CURRENT 15°C 4th
MAX 32.5°C MIN 11°C	MAX 33.5°C MIN 13°C	MAX 32°C MIN 7.5°C	MAX 29.5°C MIN 9.5°C
Starling 5	Blackbird (F)(M)	Blackbird (M)(f)	Blackbird (M)(F)
Blackbird	Starling 5	Starling 4 Woodpigeon	Starling 5
Goldfinch	Bullfinch	Magpie Robin (Audrey)	Wren
	Greenfinch	Chaffinch	Goldfinch (MF)
	Bluetit 4	Great tit	Wren 2
	Chaffinch (M)	Bluetit	Woodpigeon
	Dunnock 2	Goldfinch (MF)	Chaffinch
	Goldfinch 2 (MF)	Collared dove 2	
		Brimham	BRIMHAM

YEAR 3 CURRENT 19.5°C 1st	CURRENT 17.5°C 2nd	CURRENT 19.5°C 3rd	CURRENT 21.5°C 4th
WK 10 SUN MAX 29°C MIN 16.5°C	MAX 32.5°C MIN 10.5°C	MAX 29.5°C MIN 11.5°C	MAX 25.5°C MIN 11°C
Starling	Collared dove	Starling 4	Starling 4.6
Great tit	Goldfinch	Bullfinch 2	Blackbird 2
Greenfinch 3	Starling 2	Coal tit	Coal tit
Blackbird	Blackbird	Greenfinch	Bullfinch
Collared dove	Greenfinch	Bluetit 2	Greenfinch 2
		Collared dove 2	Great tit

JUNE

	5th	6th	7th
	Bullfinch (F)	Bluetit (2)	Blackbird
	Blackbird	Coal tit (2)	Bluetit (2)
	Wood pigeon	Starling	Collared dove 2
	Bluetit	Greenfinch	Starlings 4
	Coal tit	Wood pigeon	Dunnock
	Chaffinch (F)	Blackbird	Bullfinch (M)
	Collared dove 2	Collared dove	
	Helmsley (Malton)	Bullfinch (F)	
		(Scarborough)	

5th CURRENT 16°C MAX 17.5°C MIN 12°C
Blackbird
Bluetit 23
Starling 3
Greenfinch
Darkpigeon

6th CURRENT 14°C MAX 22°C MIN 12.5°C
Bluetit 2   Wren.
Starling 6
Collared dove
Blackbird M (F)
Bullfinch (m)
Greenfinch 56
Chaffinch (M)
Coal tit

7th CURRENT 16°C MAX 20°C MIN 12.5°C
Blackbird (M)
Bluetit 3
Starling 26
Chaffinch
Sparrow 2 (M)(FF)
Collared dove 2
Dunnock 2
Woodpigeon

5th CURRENT 17°C MAX 30.5°C MIN 13°C
Bullfinch 2
Starling 2
Goldfinch 2
Coal tit
Bluetit
Greenfinch
Woodpigeon

6th CURRENT 14°C MAX 36°C MIN 12.5°C
Collared dove 2
Starling 2
Bullfinch (M)
Bluetit
Coal tit
Greenfinch 2
Dunnock

7th CURRENT 18°C MAX 32.5°C MIN 13°C
Starling 23
Bullfinch 2
Collared dove 2
Great tit 4

Bat.
Squirrel

FA Dorothy & Ray

The whinchat, unlike its close relative the stonechat, is a non resident, with us from April until September. They favour the upland areas of Britain where they rear their young on a diet of insects. Whinchats stay together in family groups for some time after the young have left the nest.

Whinchat

JUNE

YEAR 1 2001 — 8th	9th	WK 11. Sun. — 10th	11th
Greenfinch 3	Starlings X5 Robin	Starling 2	Collared dove
Bluetit 2	Bluetit 2 Woodpigeon	Bluetit 43	Greenfinch
Robin !	Blackbird 3 Bullfinch (M)	Coal tit	Coal tit 2
Blackbird	Collared dove 2 Goldfinch	Greenfinch 3	Starling 2
Starling 2	Chaffinch (F) (M) (Immature)	Collared dove	Robin
Dunnock	Coal tit	Blackbird	Bluetit 2
Bullfinch (M)	Greenfinch	Dunnock	Bullfinch
Coal tit.	Magpie	Chaffinch	Blackbird
Collared dove 2			

YEAR 2 CURRENT 14ºC — 8th	CURRENT 19ºC SUN WK11 — 9th	CURRENT 12.5ºC — 10th	CURRENT 12.5ºC — 11th
MAX 24ºC MIN 13.5ºC	MAX 18.5ºC MIN 11.5ºC	MAX 24ºC MIN 8.5ºC	MAX 28.5ºC MIN 6ºC
Blackbird 2(Ms) Magpie	Blackbird	Blackbird (M)(F)	Blackbird
Goldfinch 2	Starling 3&6	Starling 2 Goldfinch	Bluetit
Bluetit 25	Bluetit 23	Bluetit 2	Greenfinch 2
Woodpigeon	Woodpigeon	Chaffinch (M)	Goldfinch
Chaffinch (M)(F)	Collared dove	Dunnock	
Starling 7	Greenfinch 2	Squirrel !!	
Greenfinch	Chaffinch (M)	Collared dove	
Dunnock	Great tit.	Greenfinch	Leeds + absent.

YEAR 3 CURRENT 16ºC SUN WK 11 — 8th	CURRENT 16.5ºC — 9th	CURRENT 15.5ºC — 10th	CURRENT 17ºC — 11th
MAX 29.5ºC MIN 10.5ºC	MAX 31ºC MIN 12ºC	MAX 39.5ºC MIN 13ºC	MAX 24.5ºC MIN 12ºC
Bluetit 4	Great tit.	Bluetit	Blackbird
Woodpigeon	Blackbird	Collared dove	Starling 3
Crow	Bullfinch 2	Blackbird	Bullfinch 2
Blackbird	Dunnock	Starling	Woodpigeon
			Bluetit
Cat		Grantham	

JUNE

ADDITIONAL NOTES:
Sun. June 10th Baby bluetits flew nest in afternoon. Only 1 crash landed on conservatory roof.
2003 June 8th Baby bluetit from elsewhere

The whitethroat population plummeted by approximately eighty per cent in 1969 after a drought hit their winter home, south of the Sahara. Today, although no longer our most common member of the warbler family, whitethroats can still be found each summer throughout the British Isles.

	12th	13th	14th
	2 Bluetits - young ones!	Starling 4	Bluetits 2
		Coal tit	Starling 10
		Dunnock	Blackbird
		Bullfinch (M)	Collared dove
			Wood pigeon 2
			Bullfinch (M & F)
			Greenfinch 3
	York - Dad hospital trip	York.	Dunnock.
			~~York~~

	12th	13th	14th
	CURRENT 13°C	CURRENT 13°C	CURRENT 14.5°C
	MAX 27°C MIN 10.5°C	MAX 21.5°C MIN 11°C	MAX 25°C MIN 12°C
	Blackbird	Starling 5	Blackbird
	Starling	Collared dove	Bluetit 8
	Bluetit 3	Chaffinch	Goldfinch 2
		Greenfinch	Dunnock
		Bluetit	Great tit
		Blackbird	
		Coal tit 8	
	Leeds + about.	F.A. @ YORK.	

	12th	13th	14th
	CURRENT 17°C	CURRENT 17.5°C	CURRENT 16.5°C
	MAX 28°C MIN 10.5°C	MAX 37.5°C MIN 12.5°C	MAX 42°C MIN 12.5°C
	Collared dove 2	Starling 2	Woodpigeon
	Blackbird	Bluetit 2	Greenfinch 2
	Bluetit 3	Great tit	Coal tit
	Dunnock	Bullfinch (M&F)	Bluetit 3
	Greenfinch 2	Dunnock	Dunnock
	Woodpigeon	Collared dove 2	Blackbird
	Bullfinch 2	Greenfinch 3	Collared dove 2
		Blackbird 2	

Whitethroat

JUNE

YEAR 1

15th	16th	Wk.12 Sun. 17th	18th
	Bullfinch (M&F)	Greenfinch 2 Great tit	Woodpigeon
	Goldfinch (F) Woodpigeon 3	Goldfinch (M) Jackdaw	Greenfinch 2
	Coal tit 2 Blackbird	Bluetit 23 Magpie	Collared dove
	Greenfinch 2 Dunnock	Collared dove Chaffinch	
	Bluetit	Starling 34 H. Sparrow	
	Starling 4	Bullfinch (M)	
	Collared dove	Blackbird 2	
YORK	Chaffinch (F)	Coal tit	
	Great Tit 2	YORK	YORK

YEAR 2

CURRENT 16.5°C 15th MAX 30.5°C MIN 13°C	CURRENT 18°C SUN WK12 16th MAX 26°C MIN 14.5°C	CURRENT 20°C 17th MAX 28.5°C MIN 14°C	CURRENT 19.5°C 18th MAX 29.5°C MIN 10.5°C
Starling 3	Bluetit	Woodpigeon	Blackbird (F)
Collared dove	Starling 2	Starling	Goldfinch (fledgling)
Blackbird	Blackbird	Coal tit	
Chaffinch (F)	Greenfinch	Goldfinch 2	
Bluetit	Woodpigeon	Chaffinch	
Greenfinch		Blackbird	
	BRIMHAM		FA & Helmsley

YEAR 3

SUN WK12 CURRENT 19.5°C 15th MAX 32.5°C MIN 10.5°C	CURRENT 17.5°C 16th MAX 33°C MIN 12.5°C	CURRENT 20.5°C 17th MAX 30.5°C MIN 11.5°C	CURRENT 18°C 18th MAX 29.5°C MIN 14.5°C
Bluetit 45	Starling 24	Collared dove 2	Starling 4
Blackbird	Blackbird 2	Blackbird 2	Blackbird 2
Starling 38	Dunnock	Greenfinch 2	Bluetit
Collared dove	Greenfinch 23	Chaffinch (M)	Chaffinch (M)
Greenfinch	Bluetit	Great tit	Dunnock
Bullfinch (M)	Collared dove	Dunnock	Bullfinch (M)
Woodpigeon 2	Bullfinch (F)		Collared dove
			Squirrel

JUNE

	19th	20th	21st
Starling 3 — Magpie	Starlings 5	Dunnock — Magpie
Chaffinch	Collared dove	Starling 2 — Blackbird 3
Blackbird	Greenfinch	Coal tit — Robin
Dunnock	Collared dove	Bluetit 2
Woodpigeon	Magpie	Greenfinch 5
Bluetit 2		Wood pigeon 2
Collared dove		Collared dove
Coal tit		Bullfinch (M)(MMF)
YORK	NOSTELL PRIORY	Great tit 3

	19th	20th	21st
CURRENT 15°C	CURRENT 17°C	CURRENT 16.5°C
MAX 32.5°C MIN 11.5°C	MAX 28.5°C MIN 10.5°C	MAX 22.5°C MIN 14.5°C
Starling 39	Goldfinch 2	Squirrel! — Greenfinch
Blackbird	Starling 3	Chaffinch (M) — Great tit
Woodpigeon	Collared dove	Collared dove
Goldfinch 2	Greenfinch	Starling 2
Chaffinch (M)	Blackbird (M)(F)	Bullfinch (M)
Greenfinch		Blackbird (M)
Dunnock		Bluetit
		Goldfinch 2

	19th	20th	21st
CURRENT 16.5°C	CURRENT 14.5°C	CURRENT 19.5°C
MAX 25.5°C MIN 11°C	MAX 30.5°C MIN 12.5°C	MAX 30.5°C MIN 12.5°C
Bluetit	Bluetit 5	Collared dove 2
Greenfinch 2	Blackbird 3	Blackbird 2
Great tit	Bullfinch (M)	Bluetit 3
Blackbird 2	Collared dove	Robin!
Collared dove 2	Greenfinch 2	Bullfinch (M)
Dunnock 2		Greenfinch 2
Coal tit		Dunnock 2
Woodpigeon		Squirrel Coal tit
Starling		

ADDITIONAL NOTES:

Arctic terns lay two or occasionally three eggs in a rudimentary nest on shingle beaches or short turf close to the sea. The nest colony is aggressively defended by the adult birds who 'dive-bomb' intruders, driving them from the area. Arctic terns are impressive travellers, spending the winter in the Antarctic before reaching our shores in April. They migrate south again in September, covering some 20,000 miles a year!

Arctic tern nest

JUNE

YEAR 1 — 22nd	23rd	Sun. Wk 13 — 24th	25th
Starling x10 Robin	Starling 23	Goldfinch Great tit	Goldfinch
Coal tit Woodpigeon	Robin	Blue tit ~~Collared dove 2~~	Blackbird
Dunnock Chaffinch	Blue tits 2	Coal tit	Dunnock
Blue tit x2	Greenfinch 2	Collared dove 2	Robin,
Great Tit 2	Great tit 2	Dunnock	Woodpigeon
Greenfinch	Dunnock	Starling 2	Starling
Bullfinch (M)	Jackdaw	Blackbird 2	Collared dove 2
Collared dove 2	Goldfinch (M)	Chaffinch (F)	Blue tit
Blackbird	Coal tit		Bullfinch (M)

YEAR 2 CURRENT 17.5°C — 22nd	SUN. WK13. CURRENT 14.5°C — 23rd	CURRENT 15.5°C — 24th	CURRENT 16°C — 25th
MAX 27.5°C MIN 11°C	MAX 29.5°C MIN 10°C	MAX 31°C MIN 11.5°C	MAX 28.5°C MIN 10.5°C
House Sparrow (F)	Blue tit 4 Woodpigeon 2	Blue tit ~~2~~ 3 5 Coal tit	Blue tit 4 5 6
Starling 2	Starling 3 Collared dove	Starling 2 Woodpigeon 2	Starling 3
Greenfinch	Dunnock 2 Blackbird (M+F) 2	Blackbird 2 Collared dove	Dunnock
Goldfinch 2	Wren	Dunnock Crow	Chaffinch (M)
Blue tit 2	Goldfinch (2)(M+F)	Wren H Sparrow	Goldfinch 2
Coal tit	Great tit	Chaffinch (M)	House Sparrow
Blackbird	Chaffinch (M)	Goldfinch	Greenfinch
Woodpigeon	Greenfinch	Greenfinch	Collared dove 2
Collared dove	Coal tit		Woodpigeon 2

YEAR 3 CURRENT 19.5°C WK13 SUN — 22nd	CURRENT 16°C — 23rd	CURRENT 16°C — 24th	CURRENT 17°C — 25th
MAX 33.5°C MIN 14.5°C	MAX MIN	MAX 36°C MIN 10°C	MAX 33.5°C MIN 11.5°C
Blackbird 2 Chaffinch	Blackbird 2	Blackbird	Blackbird
Dunnock Great tit	Starling 2	Dunnock 1+1=2	Starling 3
Greenfinch 3 4 H. Sparrow Dunnock	Dunnock	Blue tit 2	Woodpigeon
Coal tit 2 Woodpigeon	Blue tit 3	Great tit	Greenfinch 3
Robin	Greenfinch 3 5	H. Sparrow	Blue tit 2
Starling 3 4 5	H. Sparrow	Robin 7 9	Dunnock 2 (Ad.)
Collared dove 2	Great tit		Collared dove
Blue tit 3	Collared dove 2 7		Bullfinch (M)
Bullfinch 2 (M+F)	Bullfinch (M)		

	26th		27th		28th
Blackbird	Crow	Blackbird 2		Collared dove	
Bluetit 3	Robin	Starling 5		Blackbird 2	
Bullfinch (M)	~~Sparrowhawk~~	Woodpigeon		Dunnock	
Coal tit		Gt Tit		Bluetit	
Dunnock		Dunnock			
Starling 3		Collared dove 2			
Great tit		Bluetit 2			
Chaffinch (M)(F)		Robin			

CURRENT 15°C		CURRENT 12°C		CURRENT 10.5°C	
MAX 23.5°C MIN 8°C		MAX 23.5°C MIN 7.5°C		Blackbird	Bluetit 2
Bluetit 2 &6	H.Sparrow 2	Blackbird 2		Dunnock	Greenfinch
Blackbird	Goldfinch	Bluetit 4		Woodpigeon	
Great tit 2	Magpie	H.Sparrow		**HOLIDAY**	
Greenfinch 2		Dunnock			
Woodpigeon		Woodpigeon		**NORWAY + SWALBARD**	
Collared dove 2				**ISLANDS**	
Starling 9				Great tit	
Dunnock				Starling 4	

CURRENT 20.5°C 9.35am		CURRENT 20°C		CURRENT 14.5°C	
MAX 35.5°C MIN 14.5°C		MAX 22.5°C MIN 11°C		MAX 29°C MIN 8°C	
Bluetit 2	Bullfinch	Blackbird 2 4		Blackbird	
Blackbird 2		Bluetit 2 3+7 Bullfinch 2M		Bluetit	
Dunnock		Coal tit 3		Collared dove 4	
Starling		Great tit 2 3		Greenfinch	
Chaffinch		Starling 5		Bullfinch	
Great tit		Greenfinch 2 3		Dunnock.	
Collared dove 2 4		Dunnock 2			
Coal tit 2		Robin (M)(F)			
Greenfinch		Collared dove 2 5		Upleatham & Saltburn	

Great tit fledgling

JUNE

ADDITIONAL NOTES:

YEAR 1	29th		30th
Starling 6		Blackbird 2	Greenfinch 2
Collared dove 3		Collared dove	
Blackbirds 2		Bullfinch (M)	
Woodpigeon		Robin	
Dunnock		Bluetit 23	
		Dunnock	
		Goldfinch	
		Starling 2	

YEAR 2	29th	30th

YEAR 3	CURRENT 15°C SUN WIND 29th	CURRENT 16°C 30th
MAX 37.5°C MIN 12.5°C		MAX 13°C MIN 11°C
Greenfinch 35		Blackbird 2 Chaffinch (M)
Bluetit		Bluetit 3 Starling 3
H. Sparrow (F)		Greenfinch 35
Blackbird		Collared dove 4
Robin (fl)		Bullfinch (M)
Bullfinch (MF) 2		Great tit
Collared dove 2		Robin (fl)
Great tit 2		Dunnock 2
		Coal tit 24hrs Rain 2"

JUNE

By late June many young birds have left the nest. Some are left alone to fend for themselves, others, like this young magpie, will stay with their parents until September.

Young magpie

JULY CHECKLIST

YEAR	1	2	3
DIVERS			
Red-throated diver			
Black-throated diver			
Great Northern diver			
GREBES			
Little grebe			
Great crested grebe			
Red-necked grebe			
Slavonian grebe			
Black-necked grebe			
SHEARWATERS			
Fulmar			
Cory's shearwater			
Great shearwater			
Sooty shearwater			
Manx shearwater			
Mediterranean shearwater			
STORM PETRELS			
Storm petrel			
Leach's petrel			
GANNETS			
Gannet			
CORMORANTS			
Cormorant			
Shag			
HERONS			
Bittern			
Night heron			
Little egret			
Great white egret			
Grey heron			
Purple heron			
IBISES			
Spoonbill			
DUCKS			
Mute swan			
Bewick's swan			
Whooper swan			
Bean goose			
Pink-footed goose			
White-fronted goose			
Greylag goose			
Snow goose			
Canada goose			
Barnacle goose			
Brent goose			
Egyptian goose			
Shelduck			
Mandarin			
Wigeon			
American wigeon			
Gadwall			
Teal			
Mallard			
Pintail			
Garganey			
Shoveler			
Red-crested pochard			

YEAR	1	2	3
DUCKS (*cont.*)			
Pochard			
Ring-necked duck			
Ferruginous duck			
Tufted duck			
Scaup			
Eider			
King eider			
Long-tailed duck			
Common scoter			
Surf scoter			
Velvet scoter			
Goldeneye			
Smew			
Red-breasted merganser			
Goosander			
Ruddy duck			
HAWKS			
Honey buzzard			
Black kite			
Red kite			
White-tailed eagle			
Marsh harrier			
Hen harrier			
Montagu's harrier			
Goshawk			
Sparrowhawk			
Buzzard			
Rough-legged buzzard			
Golden eagle			
OSPREYS			
Osprey			
FALCONS			
Kestrel			
Red-footed falcon			
Merlin			
Hobby			
Peregrine			
GROUSE			
Red grouse			
Ptarmigan			
Black grouse			
Capercaillie			
PHEASANTS			
Red-legged partridge			
Grey partridge			
Quail			
Pheasant			
Golden pheasant			
Lady Amherst's pheasant			
RAILS			
Water rail			
Spotted crake			
Corncrake			
Moorhen			
Coot			
CRANES			
Crane			

YEAR	1	2	3
OYSTERCATCHERS			
Oystercatcher			
AVOCETS			
Black-winged stilt			
Avocet			
THICK-KNEES			
Stone curlew			
PLOVERS			
Little ringed plover			
Ringed plover			
Kentish plover			
Dotterel			
Golden plover			
Grey plover			
Lapwing			
Turnstone			
SANDPIPERS			
Knot			
Sanderling			
Little stint			
Temminck's stint			
White-rumped sandpiper			
Pectoral sandpiper			
Curlew sandpiper			
Purple sandpiper			
Dunlin			
Buff-breasted sandpiper			
Ruff			
Jack snipe			
Snipe			
Woodcock			
Black-tailed godwit			
Bar-tailed godwit			
Whimbrel			
Curlew			
Spotted redshank			
Redshank			
Marsh sandpiper			
Greenshank			
Green sandpiper			
Wood sandpiper			
Common sandpiper			
PHALAROPES			
Red-necked phalarope			
Grey phalarope			
SKUAS			
Pomarine skua			
Arctic skua			
Long-tailed skua			
Great skua			
GULLS			
Mediterranean gull			
Little gull			
Sabine's gull			
Black-headed gull			
Ring-billed gull			
Common gull			
Lesser black-backed gull			

YEAR	1	2	3
GULLS (*cont.*)			
Herring gull			
Iceland gull			
Glaucous gull			
Great black-backed gull			
Kittiwake			
Sandwich tern			
Roseate tern			
Common tern			
Arctic tern			
Little tern			
Black tern			
White-winged black tern			
AUKS			
Guillemot			
Razorbill			
Black guillemot			
Little auk			
Puffin			
PIGEONS			
Rock dove			
Stock dove			
Wood-pigeon	✓	✓	✓
Collared dove	✓	✓	✓
Turtle dove			
PARROTS			
Ring-necked parakeet			
CUCKOOS			
Cuckoo			
BARN OWLS			
Barn owl			
OWLS			
Snowy owl			
Little owl			
Tawny owl			
Long-eared owl			
Short-eared owl			
NIGHTJARS			
Nightjar			
SWIFTS			
Swift			
Alpine swift			
KINGFISHERS			
Kingfisher			
BEE-EATERS			
Bee-eater			
HOOPOES			
Hoopoe			
WOODPECKERS			
Wryneck			
Green woodpecker			
Great spotted woodpecker			
Lesser spotted woodpecker			
LARKS			
Short-toed lark			
Woodlark			
Skylark			
Shore lark			

YEAR	1	2
SWALLOWS		
Sand martin		
Swallow		
House martin		
PIPITS		
Richard's pipit		
Tawny pipit		
Tree pipit		
Meadow pipit		
Red-throated pipit		
Rock pipit		
Water pipit		
Yellow wagtail		
Grey wagtail		
Pied wagtail		
WAXWINGS		
Waxwing		
DIPPERS		
Dipper		
WRENS		
Wren		
ACCENTORS		
Dunnock	✓	✓
THRUSHES		
Robin	✓	
Nightingale		
Bluethroat		
Black redstart		
Redstart		
Whinchat		
Stonechat		
Wheatear		
Ring ouzel		
Blackbird	✓	✓
Fieldfare		
Song thrush		
Redwing		
Mistle thrush		✓
FLYCATCHERS		
Cetti's warbler		
Grasshopper warbler		
Savi's warbler		
Aquatic warbler		
Sedge warbler		
Marsh warbler		
Reed warbler		
Icterine warbler		
Melodious warbler		
Dartford warbler		
Subalpine warbler		
Barred warbler		
Lesser whitethroat		
Whitethroat		
Garden warbler		
Blackcap		
Pallas's warbler		
Yellow-browed warbler		
Wood warbler		

NON-LISTED SIGHTINGS

Stunningly beautiful birds, kingfishers have an almost jewel-like quality. They are shy birds, often seen only as a blue streak as they fly past at speed. The kingfisher catches its prey by diving head first into the water from its look-out perch. Sometimes, however, they can be seen hovering above the water before making a dive.

JULY

YEAR 1 2001 Sun. Wk1. Qtr 2	1st		2nd		3rd		4th
Bluetit 5	Coal tit	Woodpigeon		Collared dove 2		Chaffinch (M)(F)	
Robin 1	Woodpigeon	Blackbird 2		Blackbird 2		Blackbird 2	
Blackbird 2	Goldfinch	Bluetit		Bullfinch		Collared dove	
Starling 2,3	Bullfinch (M)(F)			Robin		Bullfinch (M)	
Dunnock 1				Woodpigeon		Starling 2	
Chaffinch 2				Bluetit 3		Greenfinch 2	
Gt. Tit 1				Greenfinch			
Greenfinch 2				Starling			
Collared dove 2		(FA + Brunham all day)		(Malton)			

YEAR 2	1st		2nd		3rd		4th

YEAR 3 CURRENT 12°C MAX 17°C MIN 12°C	1st	CURRENT 15°C MAX 22.5°C MIN 12°C	2nd	CURRENT 15.5°C MAX 22°C MIN 12°C	3rd	CURRENT 14°C MAX 33.5°C MIN 12.5°C	4th
Collared dove 2,4,5		Blackbird 2		Blackbird		Collared dove 4	
Greenfinch 2,8		Greenfinch 3,5		Greenfinch 2,3,4,5		Siskin	
Starling 2,5		Collared dove 2,3		Bluetit 4		Greenfinch 2,3	
Dunnock 3		Bluetit		Starling		Bluetit	
Bluetit		Starling 3		Collared dove		Blackbird 2 (F)(?)	
Great Tit		Bullfinch 2				Starling	
Blackbird		Siskin 1				Chaffinch (M)	
H. Sparrow 4 (F)(?) (Rain)		Dunnock					
Bullfinch (M)							

JULY

	5th	6th	7th
Squirrel !!!		
bluetit 2		
blackbird		
Greenfinch 2		
chaffinch (M)(F)		
Malton	Busy!	London

	5th	6th	7th

5th	6th	7th
CURRENT 15.5°C	CURRENT 16.0°C	CURRENT 19°C
MAX 22.5°C MIN 12.5°C	MAX 24.5°C MIN 11°C	MAX 32°C MIN 15°C
bluetit 3 4 7	Collared dove 3	Bullfinch (M) 2
blackbird	Blackbird	Starling Collared dove 2
Dunnock	bluetit 3	Dunnock
Great tit 3 4	Starling 2	Chaffinch
chaffinch 2 (M F)	H. Sparrow 3 5	bluetit 2 3
Greenfinch 2 4 5 6 8	Greenfinch 2	Great tit 2
. Sparrow 5	Chaffinch (M)	Greenfinch 2 4
collared dove 2	Great tit	H. Sparrow 2
		Coal tit

ADDITIONAL NOTES:

Before 1955 the collared dove was unknown in Britain, but it is now widespread over most of the country. Evergreen trees seem to be favoured as nest sites, although they will nest in deciduous trees and sometimes on buildings. Collared doves have been known to successfully raise five broods in a single year!

Collared dove

JULY

YEAR 1 2001 8th	9th	10th	11th
Sun, wk 2	Robin (Squirrel)		Robin (Squirrel)
	Bluetit ×5 dunnock		Bluetit
	Housesparrow (F) Greenfinch		Dunnock Woodpigeon 2
	Collared dove		Greenfinch 2
	Woodpigeon 2		Blackbird
	Great tit		Bullfinch (M)
	Chaffinch (F)(M)		Chaffinch (F)
	Bullfinch (F)		Collared dove
Hampton Court Flower Show	Starling	Matton a out in evening	(windy - squally showers)

YEAR 2 8th	9th	10th	11th

YEAR 3 CURRENT 18.5°C 8th	CURRENT (PM) 25°C 9th	CURRENT 23°C 10th	CURRENT 16°C 11th
MAX 29°C MIN 15°C	MAX 35°C MIN 16°C	MAX 35°C MIN 13°C	MAX 22.5°C MIN 12°C
H. Sparrow ×5	Greenfinch 3	Blackbird	Blackbird
Great tit 2	Dunnock	Greenfinch 2	Bluetit ×6
Bluetit ×6	Bluetit 2	Bluetit 2	Greenfinch ×3
Collared dove	Blackbird	Dunnock	Collared dove ×4
Blackbird	Collared dove	Starling ×3	Coal tit
Greenfinch 4		Collared dove ×4	Robin (F)
Coal tit		H. Sparrow 2	H. Sparrow 2
Bullfinch		Woodpigeon	
	(Out all morning)		

JULY

ADDITIONAL NOTES: 2001
11th feathers on grass - blackbird (M)??
2003 12th come back to juvenile bluetits
great tits, blackbirds, greenfinches & collared
doves - very satisfying!

	12th	13th	14th
	Bluetit	Bullfinch (M)	Greenfinch
	Blackbird	Bluetit	Blackbird
	Collared Dove 2	Chaffinch	Bluetit 2
		Collared dove 2	Great tit (young)
		Great tit	Collared dove
	(Malton)		

	12th	13th	14th SUN. WK3. CURRENT 18.5°C
		MAX 35.5°C MIN 7.5°C	MAX 33.5°C MIN 12.5°C
		(FOR 2 WKS AWAY)	Bluetit 6
			Great tit 8
			Greenfinch 4
		RETURN FROM	Dunnock
			Blackbird 2
		HOLIDAY.	Starling 3
		Collared dove 2	Chaffinch (M)
			Collared dove.

12th CURRENT 18°C	13th CURRENT 20.5°C WK 2 SUN	14th CURRENT 22°C
MAX 29.5°C MIN 12°C	MAX 40°C MIN 12°C	MAX MIN
Bluetit 3	Bluetit 3 Woodpigeon	Crow Bullfinch 2
Collared dove 2	Greenfinch 5	Bluetit 6
Blackbird	Dunnock	Great tit
Greenfinch 3	Blackbird	Collared dove
H Sparrow 3	Chaffinch	H. Sparrow 2
Bullfinch 2	Bullfinch (M)	Starling 5
36 in (FL)	H. Sparrow 3	Chaffinch (M) 2
	Great tit	Blackbird 2
	Collared dove 2	Greenfinch 4

The goldcrest is Britain's smallest bird, they suffer heavy losses in cold winters. Goldcrests overcome this problem by boosting their numbers during the breeding season. At this time of the year the female will be sitting on her second clutch of up to ten eggs, leaving the male to feed and care for their first brood.

Goldcrest

JULY

YEAR 1 200j 15th	16th	17th	18th
Sun. Wk. 3.			
Coal tit	Jackdaw	Bluetit 235	Blackbird 2
Robin	Greenfinch 24	H. Sparrow	Greenfinch 3
Bluetit 2	Blackbird 3	Greenfinch 3	Chaffinch
Blackbird 5	Bluetit 3	Collared dove	Starling
H. Sparrow 1	Goldfinch 2	Blackbird	Bullfinch (M)
Dunnock 2	House sparrow (M)(F)	Coal tit	
Chaffinch 1	Chaffinch (F)	Woodpigeon	
Great tit 2	Coal tit	Chaffinch	
Collared dove 1	Collared dove 2		

YEAR 2 CURRENT 14°° 15th	CURRENT 17°C 16th	CURRENT 18°C 17th	CURRENT 17°C 18th
MAX 26.5°C MIN 13°C	MAX 32°C MIN 13.5°C	MAX 24°C MIN 13.5°C	MAX 30°C MIN 14°C
Blackbird Collared dove	Blackbird 3	Bluetit 15 Starling	Great tit 2
Starling 3	Bluetit 8	Great tit 2 Collared dove 2	Bluetit 2
Bluetit 357	Great tit 23	Blackbird 2	Starling 2
Greenfinch D3	Collared dove 2	Greenfinch 2	Chaffinch
Chaffinch (F) 2	Greenfinch 34	Chaffinch 1	Greenfinch 2
H. Sparrow	Starling	Bullfinch 2 (MF)	
Great tit 5	H. Sparrow	Coal tit	
Bullfinch (M)	Dunnock 2	Woodpigeon	
			(York for Dad)

YEAR 3 15th	16th	17th	18th
St James Hospital			

JULY

	19th		20th		21st
Bluetit 7		Great tit		Blackbird 2	
Greenfinch 36				Bluetit 234	
Chaffinch (M)				Greenfinch	
Collared dove 2				Bullfinch (M)	
Blackbird 3				Chaffinch (M)	
Sparrow (M)				Bullfinch (M)!	
Bullfinch (M)					
		Busy!!		(Burnham after lunch)	

	19th		20th		21st
CURRENT 17°C		CURRENT 17°C		WK4.50N	
MAX 21.5°C MIN 11°C		MAX MIN		MAX 28.5°C MIN 10°C	
Blackbird 3 Dunnock 2		Bluetit 5		Woodpigeon 2	
Bluetit 10 Starling 3		Greenfinch 2		Magpie	
. Sparrow Magpie		Bullfinch (M)		Coal tit	
Collared dove 2		Great tit		Bluetit &♀	
Great tit 3				Greenfinch 3	
Chaffinch (F)6(MFY)				Bullfinch (MF)	
Bullfinch (MF) 2					
Mistle Thrush					
Greenfinch 2		CAT			

	19th		20th		21st

Headingley Hall ——————————————⟶

ADDITIONAL NOTES:
16th 2002. Young dunnock seen on roof of Lesley's house
17th At least 15 bluetits wheeling, feeding down trap 6 at a time - ba they in biding th along with 2 great tits, 2 bullfinches + chaffinch!
19th Thrush first time for ages
19th 2002. F. Bullfinch among M offspring.
'' Family of 6 chaffinches M, F & 4 Y

Gannets nest in large, noisy colonies, usually on offshore rocky islands. They communicate with their partners by using a complex system of gestures: bowing, sky pointing, neck biting etc. Illustrated here is the mutual fencing display, which each pair use as part of their greeting ceremony.

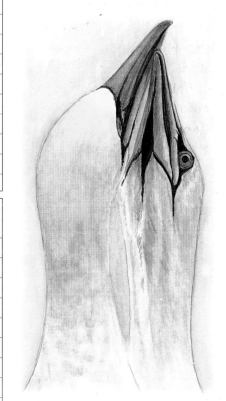

Gannets

JULY

YEAR 1	22nd	23rd	24th	25t
Brimham		Brimham ½ day	Brimham	Brimham

YEAR 2	22nd	23rd	24th	25
CURRENT 16.5°C MAX 19.5°C MIN 14°C	CURRENT 17.5°C MAX 22°C MIN 10.5°C	CURRENT 15°C MAX MIN		
Bluetit 12 Thrush	Dunnock Starling	Greenfinch 7		
Greenfinch 36 ~~Dunnocks 3~~	Bluetit 58	Bluetit 2		
Great tit 3	Greenfinch 8	Collared dove		
Blackbird	Great tit 2			
Crow	Blackbird 3			
Dunnocks 3	Coal tit			
Collared dove	Collared dove 4			
Coal tit	Woodpigeon			
Squirrel		Brimham	Brimham	

YEAR 3	22nd	23rd	24th	25

JULY

26th	27th	28th
Brimham	Brimham	Brimham

26th	27th Wk. 5 Sun.	28th
	MAX 39°C	MIN 12.5°C
Brimham	Brimham	Brimham

26th	27th	28th

The golden plover spends its summer on the upland moors where it breeds. Both sexes form nest scrapes, one of which is chosen by the female. She lines it with twigs, lichen and grass before laying a clutch of three or four eggs.

Golden plover

JULY

Extremely hot weather 25°C – 30°C from 23rd July to 1st Aug. inclusive

YEAR 1	29th		30th		31st
SUN WK5					
		Collared dove			
		Blackbird			
Branham		Branham		Branham	

YEAR 2 CURRENT 21.5°C	29th	CURRENT 22°C	30th	CURRENT 16.5°C	31st
MAX 36°C MIN 17.5°C		MAX 26°C MIN 15°C		MAX 20.5°C MIN 15.5°C	
Bluetit 2		Blackbird 3		Greenfinch ≥ 10	
Greenfinch ≥ 6		Bluetit 2		Bluetits ≥ 12	
Crow		Greenfinch 2		Blackbird	
Collared dove 2.		Collared dove 2		Starling 2	
				Collared dove 2	
				Dunnock 2	
				~~Coaltit~~	
		Thunderstorms Violent rain		Rain, Fog.	

YEAR 3	29th		30th		31st

JULY

The streets of London were once scavenged by red kites. By 1900 these magnificent birds had been persecuted almost to the point of extinction. Only a few pairs were left, in the remote valleys of mid-Wales. Today, thanks to a well organised reintroduction programme, red kites are slowly increasing in numbers.

Red kite

AUGUST CHECKLIST

DIVERS
- Red-throated diver
- Black-throated diver
- Great Northern diver

GREBES
- Little grebe
- Great crested grebe
- Red-necked grebe
- Slavonian grebe
- Black-necked grebe

SHEARWATERS
- Fulmar
- Cory's shearwater
- Great shearwater
- Sooty shearwater
- Manx shearwater
- Mediterranean shearwater

STORM PETRELS
- Storm petrel
- Leach's petrel

GANNETS
- Gannet

CORMORANTS
- Cormorant
- Shag

HERONS
- Bittern
- Night heron
- Little egret
- Great white egret
- Grey heron
- Purple heron

IBISES
- Spoonbill

DUCKS
- Mute swan
- Bewick's swan
- Whooper swan
- Bean goose
- Pink-footed goose
- White-fronted goose
- Greylag goose
- Snow goose
- Canada goose
- Barnacle goose
- Brent goose
- Egyptian goose
- Shelduck
- Mandarin
- Wigeon
- American wigeon
- Gadwall
- Teal
- Mallard
- Pintail
- Garganey
- Shoveler
- Red-crested pochard

DUCKS (*cont.*)
- Pochard
- Ring-necked duck
- Ferruginous duck
- Tufted duck
- Scaup
- Eider
- King eider
- Long-tailed duck
- Common scoter
- Surf scoter
- Velvet scoter
- Goldeneye
- Smew
- Red-breasted merganser
- Goosander
- Ruddy duck

HAWKS
- Honey buzzard
- Black kite
- Red kite
- White-tailed eagle
- Marsh harrier
- Hen harrier
- Montagu's harrier
- Goshawk
- Sparrowhawk
- Buzzard
- Rough-legged buzzard
- Golden eagle

OSPREYS
- Osprey

FALCONS
- Kestrel
- Red-footed falcon
- Merlin
- Hobby
- Peregrine

GROUSE
- Red grouse
- Ptarmigan
- Black grouse
- Capercaillie

PHEASANTS
- Red-legged partridge
- Grey partridge
- Quail
- Pheasant
- Golden pheasant
- Lady Amherst's pheasant

RAILS
- Water rail
- Spotted crake
- Corncrake
- Moorhen
- Coot

CRANES
- Crane

OYSTERCATCHERS
- Oystercatcher

AVOCETS
- Black-winged stilt
- Avocet

THICK-KNEES
- Stone curlew

PLOVERS
- Little ringed plover
- Ringed plover
- Kentish plover
- Dotterel
- Golden plover
- Grey plover
- Lapwing
- Turnstone

SANDPIPERS
- Knot
- Sanderling
- Little stint
- Temminck's stint
- White-rumped sandpiper
- Pectoral sandpiper
- Curlew sandpiper
- Purple sandpiper
- Dunlin
- Buff-breasted sandpiper
- Ruff
- Jack snipe
- Snipe
- Woodcock
- Black-tailed godwit
- Bar-tailed godwit
- Whimbrel
- Curlew
- Spotted redshank
- Redshank
- Marsh sandpiper
- Greenshank
- Green sandpiper
- Wood sandpiper
- Common sandpiper

PHALAROPES
- Red-necked phalarope
- Grey phalarope

SKUAS
- Pomarine skua
- Arctic skua
- Long-tailed skua
- Great skua

GULLS
- Mediterranean gull
- Little gull
- Sabine's gull
- Black-headed gull
- Ring-billed gull
- Common gull
- Lesser black-backed gull

GULLS (*cont.*)
- Herring gull
- Iceland gull
- Glaucous gull
- Great black-backed gull
- Kittiwake
- Sandwich tern
- Roseate tern
- Common tern
- Arctic tern
- Little tern
- Black tern
- White-winged black tern

AUKS
- Guillemot
- Razorbill
- Black guillemot
- Little auk
- Puffin

PIGEONS
- Rock dove
- Stock dove
- Wood-pigeon — 2 ✓ 3 ✓
- Collared dove — 1 ✓ 2 ✓ 3 ✓
- Turtle dove

PARROTS
- Ring-necked parakeet

CUCKOOS
- Cuckoo

BARN OWLS
- Barn owl

OWLS
- Snowy owl
- Little owl
- Tawny owl
- Long-eared owl
- Short-eared owl

NIGHTJARS
- Nightjar

SWIFTS
- Swift
- Alpine swift

KINGFISHERS
- Kingfisher

BEE-EATERS
- Bee-eater

HOOPOES
- Hoopoe

WOODPECKERS
- Wryneck
- Green woodpecker
- Great spotted woodpecker
- Lesser spotted woodpecker

LARKS
- Short-toed lark
- Woodlark
- Skylark
- Shore lark

SWALLOWS
- Sand martin
- Swallow
- House martin

PIPITS
- Richard's pipit
- Tawny pipit
- Tree pipit
- Meadow pipit
- Red-throated pipit
- Rock pipit
- Water pipit
- Yellow wagtail
- Grey wagtail
- Pied wagtail

WAXWINGS
- Waxwing

DIPPERS
- Dipper

WRENS
- Wren

ACCENTORS
- Dunnock — 1 ✓ 2 ✓ 3 ✓

THRUSHES
- Robin — 1 ✓ 2 ✓ 3 ✓
- Nightingale
- Bluethroat
- Black redstart
- Redstart
- Whinchat
- Stonechat
- Wheatear
- Ring ouzel
- Blackbird — 1 ✓ 2 ✓
- Fieldfare — 2 ✓
- Song thrush — 2 ✓
- Redwing
- Mistle thrush

FLYCATCHERS
- Cetti's warbler
- Grasshopper warbler
- Savi's warbler
- Aquatic warbler
- Sedge warbler
- Marsh warbler
- Reed warbler
- Icterine warbler
- Melodious warbler
- Dartford warbler
- Subalpine warbler
- Barred warbler
- Lesser whitethroat
- Whitethroat
- Garden warbler
- Blackcap
- Pallas's warbler
- Yellow-browed warbler
- Wood warbler

YEAR	1	2	3
FLYCATCHERS (*cont.*)			
Chiffchaff			
Willow warbler			
Goldcrest			
Firecrest			
Spotted flycatcher			
Red-breasted flycatcher			
Pied flycatcher			
REEDLINGS			
Bearded tit			
TITMICE			
Long-tailed tit		✓	
Marsh tit			
Willow tit			
Crested tit			
Coal tit	✓	✓	✓
Blue tit	✓	✓	✓
Great tit	✓	✓	✓
NUTHATCHES			
Nuthatch			
CREEPERS			
Treecreeper			
ORIOLES			
Golden oriole			
SHRIKES			
Red-backed shrike			
Great Grey shrike			
Woodchat shrike			
CROWS			
Jay			
Magpie		✓	✓
Chough			
Jackdaw	✓	✓	
Rook			
Carrion crow			
Raven			
STARLINGS			
Starling		✓	✓
SPARROWS			
House sparrow		✓	
Tree sparrow			
BUNTINGS			
Lapland bunting			
Snow bunting			
Yellowhammer			
Girl bunting			
Ortolan bunting			
Little bunting			
Reed bunting			
Corn bunting			
FINCHES			
Chaffinch	✓	✓	✓
Brambling			
Serin			
Greenfinch	✓	✓	✓
Goldfinch			
Siskin			
Linnet			

YEAR	1	2	3
FINCHES (*cont.*)			
Twite			
Redpoll			
Arctic redpoll			
Crossbill			
Scottish crossbill			
Scarlet rosefinch			
Bullfinch	✓	✓	✓
Hawfinch			

NON-LISTED SIGHTINGS

Herons are expert fishermen, patiently surveying the surface of the water, waiting for prey to come within reach of their dagger-sharp bills. Fish are by no means the only item on their menu; small mammals, reptiles, amphibians, insects and birds are also eaten.

AUGUST

YEAR 1 2001 1st	2nd	3rd	4th
Chaffinch Blackbird 2 Bluetit	Magpie	Collared dove	Bluetit 3+4 Collared dove Greenfinch 2 Great Tit
(F.A)	(Malton)		

2002 YEAR 2 CURRENT 16.5°C 1st MAX 19.5°C MIN 14.5°C	CURRENT 14.5°C 2nd MAX 30°C MIN 11°C	CURRENT 17.5°C 3rd MAX 41°C MIN 15°C	CURRENT 18°C Sun Wk 4th MAX 24°C MIN 12.5°C
Greenfinch 5 Bluetit 25 Dunnock Coal tit Starling Great tit Blackbird Collared dove 2	Collared dove 2&4 Coal tit Bluetit 35 Chaffinch Greenfinch 26 Blackbird 2 Starling 2 Great tit Bullfinch	Greenfinch 56 Collared dove H. Sparrow 2	Collared dove Greenfinch 25 Coal tit Bluetit 13 Blackbird (M)

YEAR 3 1st	2nd	SUN WK 6 3rd	4th
		Blackbird 2 Dunnock 4 Bluetit 6 Coal tit Collared dove 2 Chaffinch 3 H. Sparrow Starling Magpie	Collared dove 2 H. Sparrow 3 Dunnock Bluetit 2 Coal tit Bullfinch lge o sm Starling white butterfly Robin

AUGUST

SUN. WK. 6 — 5th	6th	7th
Greenfinch	Greenfinch ♀4	Blackbird
Great Tit	Dunnock	Bluetit ♀3
Chaffinch (M)	Bluetit 2	Greenfinch 2
Bluetit	Blackbird	
Collared dove	Chaffinch (M)	
	Collared dove	
	Robin	
Sunny	(Rain + mist all day)	Malton

CURRENT 18°C — 5th	CURRENT 19°C — 6th	CURRENT 21°C — 7th
MAX 30.5°C MIN 14.5°C	MAX 32.5°C MIN 14.5°C	MAX 27.5°C MIN 15°C
Greenfinch 3	Bluetit ♂45	Bluetit ♀3
Collared dove	Greenfinch ♀4	Dunnock
Coal tit	Collared dove 2	Greenfinch 3
Blackbird (M)	H. Sparrow 3	Coal tit
Bluetit ♀3	Coal tit	Blackbird
Great tit	Dunnock	Collared dove
Long tailed tit 2	Blackbird (F)	~~Do~~
Song thrush		
Dunnock		

5th	6th	7th
Greenfinch	Blackbird 4	Greenfinch
Bluetit 3	Starling	Bluetit ♀9
H. Sparrow ♀3	Greenfinch 2	Collared dove ♀4
Dunnock 3	Crow 2	Chaffinch 2
Starling	Collared dove 2	Dunnock 2
Collared dove	Bluetit 2	H. Sparrow 3
Blackbird 4	H. Sparrow ♀4	Great tit
Great tit	Dunnock	Magpie
	Robin	

Green woodpeckers can often be seen on the ground feeding on ants, one of their favourite foods. They are handsome birds with a distinctive laughing call, which is said to be the origin of their country name of the 'Yaffle'.

Green woodpecker

AUGUST

YEAR 1	8th	9th	10th	11th
Bluetit 8	Bluetit	Chaffinch	Collared dove 2
Great Tit 2	Coal tit	Collared dove 2	Greenfinch 35
Greenfinch 2	Chaffinch	Greenfinch 23	Bluetit 23
Collared dove 3	Greenfinch 814	Bluetit 23	Great tit
Coal tit		Great tit 2	Coal tit

YEAR 2 CURRENT 14·5°C 8th	CURRENT 15·5°C 9th	CURRENT 12·5°C 10th	CURRENT 20·5 Sun Wk 7 11th
MAX 22·5°C MIN 12·5°C	MAX 22·5°C MIN 11·5°C	MAX 21·5°C MIN 12·5°C	MAX 28°C MIN 13·5°C
Robin (Fled)	Collared dove 23	Collared dove 23	Blackbird (F)(M)
Coal tit	Dunnock	Bluetit	Greenfinch 234
Bluetit 2	Starling		Song Thrush
Chaffinch (F)	Bluetit 8311		Dunnock 2
Greenfinch 2	Greenfinch 84		Coal tit
Collared dove 2	Coal tit		Bluetit 4
Blackbird 2	Great tit		
Dunnock 3	Sparrow		
Starling	Blackbird 2 (Rain all day)	Rain Helmsley/ Beadlam	Dull - Showery

YEAR 3	8th	9th	Sun Wk 7 10th	11th
Bluetit 87	Bluetit 2	Bluetit 2	Bullfinch (F)
H. Sparrow 24	Dunnock	H. Sparrow 2	Bluetit 3
Dunnock	Greenfinch	Dunnock	Collared dove 2
Collared dove 2	H. Sparrow 4	Collared dove 23	Dunnock
Chaffinch 2	Collared dove 2	Bullfinch (F)(M)	Starling
Greenfinch 2 Peacock Bfly		Greenfinch 2	
Robin		Coal tit	
Siskin (F)			

AUGUST

8th Fledgling robin! 2002
14th 2002 3 Fieldfares visited Rowan tree
12th 2003 Mixed flock G.finch, B.tit & H.Sparrow

Storm petrels are true sea-birds, only coming ashore in the breeding season. They feed on plankton and other marine life, brought to the surface by the action of the waves. On calm seas they appear to walk on the water, as they 'patter' across its surface looking for food.

	12th	13th	14th
SUN LOC ?			
	Chaffinch 2	Blue tit	Collared dove 2
	G. Tit	Great Tit	Greenfinch 23
	Blue tit	Greenfinch 2	Blue tit
	Greenfinch 2	Collared dove 3	
	Collared dove.		

	12th	13th	14th
CURRENT 15°C	CURRENT 19.5°C	CURRENT 20.5°C	
MAX 35°C MIN 14.5°C	MAX 31°C MIN 16.5°C	MAX 36.5°C MIN 16°C	
	Greenfinch 2	Collared dove 2	Chaffinch
	Collared dove	Greenfinch 3	Greenfinch 2
	Blue tit	Robin (mature)	Blackbird
	Coal tit	Blue tit 23	Collared dove
	Great tit	H. Sparrow	Wood pigeon 2
			Sparrow
			Blue tit 2
			Fieldfare 3
YORK.	SCARBOROUGH		

	12th	13th	14th
	Dunnock	Greenfinch 3	Collared dove 2
	Collared dove	Great tit	Blue tit
	Greenfinch (8) All came	Blue tit 59	Greenfinch 3
	Blue tit (10) together in	White Pigeon	Dunnock
	H.Sparrow (8) big flock	Dunnock	Chaffinch
	Blackbird 2	Blackbird 2 & 4	White dove
	Collared dove 3	Mistle thrush Painted	Coal tit
	Great tit	Coal tit lady.	

Storm petrel

AUGUST

YEAR 1 15th	16th	17th	18th
Bluetit 6	Bluetit 5	Greenfinch 23	Robin
Greenfinch 4	Collared dove 2	Bluetit 4	Bluetit
Collared dove 2	Chaffinch	Dunnock	~~Collared doves~~
Chaffinch	Greenfinch 4	Collared dove	
	Great Tit	Coal tit	
	Blackbird	Great tit	
	Coal tit	Blackbird 2	

YEAR 2 CURRENT 19.5°C 15th	CURRENT 16°C 16th	CURRENT 21.5°C 17th	SUN WK8 CURRENT 22.5° 18th
MAX 28°C MIN 10°C	MAX 41°C MIN 15°C	MAX 36°C MIN 15.5°C	MAX 36.5°C MIN 13.5°C
Blackbird (M)	Collared dove 2	Collared dove	Bluetit
Greenfinch 27	Bluetit 24	Robin (F) 2 (MF)	Magpie
H. Sparrow	Greenfinch 5	Bluetit	Collared dove
Bluetit	Robin (F)	Greenfinch	Greenfinch
	Blackbird		
		Helmsley	

YEAR 3 15th	16th	SUN WK8 17th	18th
Collared dove 2	Greenfinch 234	Collared dove 2	Bullfinch
Bluetit 56	Bluetit	Bluetit	Bluetit
Coal tit	Coal tit	Dunnock 2	H. Sparrow
Starling	Starling	Blackbird 2	Greenfinch
Blackbird	Blackbird 2	Coal tit	Collared dove 2
Greenfinch 2	Dunnock	Great tit	White dove
Chaffinch (M)(F) 2	H. Sparrow	Greenfinch 3	
Dunnock		Bullfinch (F)(M)	
H. Sparrow		H. Sparrow	

AUGUST

SUN · WK 8	19th	20th	21st
Coal tit	Dunnock	Greenfinch 3	
Greenfinch 2,5	Bluetit 2	Bluetit	
Collared dove 2		Blackbird	
Bluetit 4			
Great tit			
		Hot - Mallon	

CURRENT 16.5°C 19th	CURRENT 17°C 20th	CURRENT 15°C 21st
MAX 26°C MIN 16.5°C	MAX 29°C MIN 10°C	MAX 40°C MIN 11°C
Blackbird (F) 2 (M,F)	Greenfinch 4	Collared dove 3
Greenfinch 5,6	Collared dove	Dunnock 2
Magpie	Bluetit	Greenfinch 2
Collared dove 2	Woodpigeon	Bluetit 2
Bluetit 2	Blackbird (M)	Great tit
		Blackbird (F)
		(FA am)

19th	20th	21st
Blackbird 2 Great tit	Bullfinch (M) Collared dove 5	Dunnock
Collared dove 2	Sparrow 2 White dove	Bluetit
Bluetit	Bluetit 2	H. Sparrow
Dunnock	Greenfinch 3	Greenfinch 3
Greenfinch 2	Dunnock	Bullfinch
Chaffinch	Chaffinch	White Dove
Sparrow	Coal tit	Woodpigeon
Bullfinch (M)	Great tit	
Coal tit	Blackbird 2	

The turnstone breeds around the coasts of Scandinavia; however non-breeding birds can be seen on British shores all year. The birds are aptly named, turning over stones, sea-weed, shells and drift-wood in their search for food.

Turnstone

AUGUST

YEAR 1

22nd	23rd	24th	25th
Bluetit 2	Coal tit	Greenfinch	Greenfinch
Dunnock	Bluetit	Bluetit	Bluetit
Greenfinch 2	Greenfinch		
Coal tit	Dunnock.		
Hot.		(Cole)	

YEAR 2

CURRENT 17°C 22nd	CURRENT 15.5°C 23rd	CURRENT 19°C 24th	CURRENT 16.5°C WK 9 SUN 25th
MAX 28°C MIN 14°C	MAX 23°C MIN 13°C	MAX 26°C MIN 13.5°C	MAX 36°C MIN 9°C
Greenfinch 8	Collared dove 3	Robin	Collared dove 2
Great tit	Greenfinch 6	Bluetit 6	Woodpigeon
Bluetit 12	Chaffinch (M)	Collared dove 24	Greenfinch 5 78
Chaffinch	Bluetit 4	Greenfinch 4	Great tit 2
Robin 2	H. Sparrow (m)	Chaffinch (F)	Bluetit
Starling 2	Robin	Great tit	H. Sparrow
Blackbird	Magpie 2	Blackbird (F)	
Collared dove		Coal tit	
		Bullfinch 2 (MF)	Brimham)

YEAR 3

22nd	Sun lok 23rd	Sun lok 9 24th	25th
Dunnock 2	White dove	White dove Crow	Bluetit 6
Greenfinch 4	unknown dove/pigeon	unknown pigeon/dove Blackbird	Coal tit
Great tit	Chaffinch	Chaffinch 23	Blackbird 2
Chaffinch		Greenfinch 3	Dunnock 2
Coal tit		Coal tit	Greenfinch 2
Blackbird 2		Great tit 2	Chaffinch 2
Blackbird		Dunnock 2	Collared dove
H. Sparrow 3		Magpie 2	
Bluetit 2		Bluetit 2	

AUGUST

	26th		27th		28th
Blue tit 2		Greenfinch 3		Bullfinch (M)	
Great Tit				Blue tit 2	
Greenfinch				Collared dove	
(Brimham) hot		(Brimham) hot			

	26th		27th		28th
CURRENT 14°C		CURRENT 16.5°C			
MAX 31.5°C MIN 10.5°C		MAX MIN			
Collared dove		Greenfinch 6	Collared dove 2		
Greenfinch 3&12		Blue tit 2	Dunnock		
Blue tit		Coal tit			
Chaffinch (M)		Great tit			
Blackbird (F)		Chaffinch (F)			
H. Sparrow		Blackbird (M)			
Siskin		Robin			
		H. Sparrow 3			
Brimham)		RUGBY PM		RUGBY	

	26th		27th		28th
Robin Blue tit		Greenfinch 2		Chaffinch	
Dunnock 2		Dunnock 3		H. Sparrow	
Blackbird 2		Collared dove 2		Blue tit	
Greenfinch 2		Blackbird		Collared dove 25	
Collared dove		Blue tit 2		Coal tit	
Chaffinch		Chaffinch		Greenfinch 4	
Coal tit		Great tit		Blackbird	
Great tit		Bullfinch (F)		Dunnock 2	
H. Sparrow 3				Great tit	

ADDITIONAL NOTES:
26th 2002 Young or female siskin. 1st time in summer.

The parties of screaming swifts that circle our roof-tops, will be leaving us soon, returning to Africa for the winter. They will now spend a staggering nine months in flight. They will not land again until they rejoin us in late April next year, to start the new breeding season.

Swifts

AUGUST

30th Mixed flock of 30/40 Blu
Greenfinch @ 9am. 2802

YEAR 1	29th	30th	31st
		Bluetit 3	Bluetit 23
		Great tit	Great tit
		Greenfinch 3	
		Dunnock	
		Chaffinch	
		Collared dove	
Malton / Helmsley / Out /			

YEAR 2	3days	29th	CURRENT 13°C	30th	CURRENT 11°C 5°C	31st
MAX 27°C MIN 9°C		MAX 27°C MIN 9°C		MAX 27°C 23°C MIN 9°C	
		Greenfinch 12 (Est)		Bluetit 3 Robin	
		Bluetit 20 (Est)		Greenfinch 4 5° Collared dove	
		Great Tit. 2		Blackbird 2 Dunnock 2	
				Magpie	
				Bullfinch (F)	
				Coal tit	
				Collared dove	
				H. Sparrow	
RUGBY				Chaffinch (M)(F)	

YEAR 3	29th	30th SUN LOW 10.	31st
Collared dove 2	Bluetit 2	Chaffinch
Greenfinch 3 4	Blackbird	Greenfinch 4
Chaffinch	Greenfinch 4	Dunnock
H. Sparrow	Dunnock 2	Blackbird
Dunnock 2	Chaffinch 2	Coal tit
Chaffinch	H. Sparrow 2	Blackbird 2
	Collared dove	Collared dove
	Robin	

AUGUST

Black-tailed godwits have recently started breeding in Britain again, after an absence of more than a hundred years. The illustration shows an adult in summer. Later in the year the birds adopt a less colourful winter plumage, with mottled brown upperparts.

Black-tailed godwit

SEPTEMBER CHECKLIST

YEAR	1	2	3
DIVERS			
Red-throated diver			
Black-throated diver			
Great Northern diver			
GREBES			
Little grebe			
Great crested grebe			
Red-necked grebe			
Slavonian grebe			
Black-necked grebe			
SHEARWATERS			
Fulmar			
Cory's shearwater			
Great shearwater			
Sooty shearwater			
Manx shearwater			
Mediterranean shearwater			
STORM PETRELS			
Storm petrel			
Leach's petrel			
GANNETS			
Gannet			
CORMORANTS			
Cormorant			
Shag			
HERONS			
Bittern			
Night heron			
Little egret			
Great white egret			
Grey heron			
Purple heron			
IBISES			
Spoonbill			
DUCKS			
Mute swan			
Bewick's swan			
Whooper swan			
Bean goose			
Pink-footed goose			
White-fronted goose			
Greylag goose			
Snow goose			
Canada goose			
Barnacle goose			
Brent goose			
Egyptian goose			
Shelduck			
Mandarin			
Wigeon			
American wigeon			
Gadwall			
Teal			
Mallard			
Pintail			
Garganey			
Shoveler			
Red-crested pochard			

YEAR	1	2	3
DUCKS (cont.)			
Pochard			
Ring-necked duck			
Ferruginous duck			
Tufted duck			
Scaup			
Eider			
King eider			
Long-tailed duck			
Common scoter			
Surf scoter			
Velvet scoter			
Goldeneye			
Smew			
Red-breasted merganser			
Goosander			
Ruddy duck			
HAWKS			
Honey buzzard			
Black kite			
Red kite			
White-tailed eagle			
Marsh harrier			
Hen harrier			
Montagu's harrier			
Goshawk			
Sparrowhawk			
Buzzard			
Rough-legged buzzard			
Golden eagle			
OSPREYS			
Osprey			
FALCONS			
Kestrel			
Red-footed falcon			
Merlin			
Hobby			
Peregrine			
GROUSE			
Red grouse			
Ptarmigan			
Black grouse			
Capercaillie			
PHEASANTS			
Red-legged partridge			
Grey partridge			
Quail			
Pheasant			
Golden pheasant			
Lady Amherst's pheasant			
RAILS			
Water rail			
Spotted crake			
Corncrake			
Moorhen			
Coot			
CRANES			
Crane			

YEAR	1	2	3
OYSTERCATCHERS			
Oystercatcher			
AVOCETS			
Black-winged stilt			
Avocet			
THICK-KNEES			
Stone curlew			
PLOVERS			
Little ringed plover			
Ringed plover			
Kentish plover			
Dotterel			
Golden plover			
Grey plover			
Lapwing			
Turnstone			
SANDPIPERS			
Knot			
Sanderling			
Little stint			
Temminck's stint			
White-rumped sandpiper			
Pectoral sandpiper			
Curlew sandpiper			
Purple sandpiper			
Dunlin			
Buff-breasted sandpiper			
Ruff			
Jack snipe			
Snipe			
Woodcock			
Black-tailed godwit			
Bar-tailed godwit			
Whimbrel			
Curlew			
Spotted redshank			
Redshank			
Marsh sandpiper			
Greenshank			
Green sandpiper			
Wood sandpiper			
Common sandpiper			
PHALAROPES			
Red-necked phalarope			
Grey phalarope			
SKUAS			
Pomarine skua			
Arctic skua			
Long-tailed skua			
Great skua			
GULLS			
Mediterranean gull			
Little gull			
Sabine's gull			
Black-headed gull			
Ring-billed gull			
Common gull			
Lesser black-backed gull			

YEAR	1	2	3
GULLS (cont.)			
Herring gull			
Iceland gull			
Glaucous gull			
Great black-backed gull			
Kittiwake			
Sandwich tern			
Roseate tern			
Common tern			
Arctic tern			
Little tern			
Black tern			
White-winged black tern			
AUKS			
Guillemot			
Razorbill			
Black guillemot			
Little auk			
Puffin			
PIGEONS			
Rock dove			
Stock dove			
Wood-pigeon	✓	✓	✓
Collared dove	✓	✓	✓
Turtle dove			
PARROTS			
Ring-necked parakeet			
CUCKOOS			
Cuckoo			
BARN OWLS			
Barn owl			
OWLS			
Snowy owl			
Little owl			
Tawny owl			
Long-eared owl			
Short-eared owl			
NIGHTJARS			
Nightjar			
SWIFTS			
Swift			
Alpine swift			
KINGFISHERS			
Kingfisher			
BEE-EATERS			
Bee-eater			
HOOPOES			
Hoopoe			
WOODPECKERS			
Wryneck			
Green woodpecker			
Great spotted woodpecker.			
Lesser spotted woodpecker			
LARKS			
Short-toed lark			
Woodlark			
Skylark			
Shore lark			

YEAR	1	2
SWALLOWS		
Sand martin		
Swallow		
House martin		
PIPITS		
Richard's pipit		
Tawny pipit		
Tree pipit		
Meadow pipit		
Red-throated pipit		
Rock pipit		
Water pipit		
Yellow wagtail		
Grey wagtail		
Pied wagtail		
WAXWINGS		
Waxwing		
DIPPERS		
Dipper		
WRENS		
Wren		
ACCENTORS		
Dunnock	✓	✓
THRUSHES		
Robin	✓	
Nightingale		
Bluethroat		
Black redstart		
Redstart		
Whinchat		
Stonechat		
Wheatear		
Ring ouzel		
Blackbird		
Fieldfare		
Song thrush		
Redwing		
Mistle thrush	✓	
FLYCATCHERS		
Cetti's warbler		
Grasshopper warbler		
Savi's warbler		
Aquatic warbler		
Sedge warbler		
Marsh warbler		
Reed warbler		
Icterine warbler		
Melodious warbler		
Dartford warbler		
Subalpine warbler		
Barred warbler		
Lesser whitethroat		
Whitethroat		
Garden warbler		
Blackcap		
Pallas's warbler		
Yellow-browed warbler		
Wood warbler		

YEAR	1	2	3
FLYCATCHERS (*cont.*)			
Chiffchaff			
Willow warbler			
Goldcrest			
Firecrest			
Spotted flycatcher			
Red-breasted flycatcher			
Pied flycatcher			
BEARDLINGS			
Bearded tit			
TITMICE			
Long-tailed tit	✓		
Marsh tit			
Willow tit			
Crested tit			
Coal tit	✓		✓
Blue tit	✓	✓	✓
Great tit	✓		✓
NUTHATCHES			
Nuthatch			
TREECREEPERS			
Treecreeper			
ORIOLES			
Golden oriole			
SHRIKES			
Red-backed shrike			
Great Grey shrike			
Woodchat shrike			
CROWS			
Magpie	✓		✓
Chough			
Jackdaw			
Rook			
Carrion crow			
Raven			
STARLINGS			
Starling	✓		
SPARROWS			
House sparrow		✓	✓
Tree sparrow			
BUNTINGS			
Lapland bunting			
Snow bunting			
Yellowhammer			
Cirl bunting			
Ortolan bunting			
Little bunting			
Reed bunting			
Corn bunting			
FINCHES			
Chaffinch	✓	✓	✓
Brambling			
Serin			
Greenfinch	✓	✓	✓
Goldfinch			
Siskin			
Linnet			

YEAR	1	2	3
FINCHES (*cont.*)			
Twite			
Redpoll			
Arctic redpoll			
Crossbill			
Scottish crossbill			
Scarlet rosefinch			
Bullfinch	✓		
Hawfinch			

NON-LISTED SIGHTINGS

The tawny owl is found over much of Britain but is absent from Ireland. Its familiar hooting call and rounded face, have made it the model for the 'wise old owls' of children's literature and folklore.

SEPTEMBER

YEAR 1 1st	SUN. WK10. 2nd	3rd	4th
Collared dove 2 dunnock Great Tit Robin Bluetit 3 Greenfinch 5 Chaffinch Coal tit	Bluetit 4 ✓ Collared dove 2 Greenfinch 3 Great tit 1 Chaffinch Coal tit Brinham	Bluetit 4 5 Collared dove Chaffinch Great tit 2 Greenfinch 2 Coal tit Long tailed tit 4	Collared dove 2 Bluetit 3 Dunnock 2 Greenfinch 4 Great tit Mistle thrush 2 Starling 4 Bullfinch

YEAR 2 WK10 SUN CURRENT 18°C 41°C 10°C 1st MAX 23°C MIN 5°C	WK10 SUN CURRENT 16°C 2nd MAX 31.5°C MIN 12.5°C	CURRENT 16°C 3rd MAX 39.5°C MIN 11.5°C	CURRENT 15.5°C 4th MAX 26°C MIN 12.5°C
Bluetit 1 Blackbird Greenfinch 3 Collared dove Dunnock Chaffinch (1M) Coal tit	Collared dove Dunnock Greenfinch 3 F. A. Deer Poole	Collared dove Greenfinch 12 Chaffinch 2 (MF) Dunnock H. Sparrow 3 Bluetit Robin Magpie	Bluetit 2 Greenfinch 4 Collared dove Great tit 2

YEAR 3 1st	2nd	3rd	4th
Bluetit 10 Greenfinch 6 Great Tit 2 Coal tit Robin	Blackbird 2 Chaffinch Greenfinch 3 Robin Bluetit 2 Dunnock Great tit	Chaffinch Greenfinch 6 Bluetit Great tit Robin Dunnock	Robin Dunnock Greenfinch 5 Bluetit Chaffinch

SEPTEMBER

1st 2003 large mixed flock of 20+
greenfinch, Bluetit coaltit a gt. Tit/open
5th 2003 Jay at top of tree with nut
in beak around 8.30am.

5th / 6th / 7th

5th		6th	7th
Dunnock	Bullfinch (M)	Greenfinch 2	Greenfinch 24
Chaffinch 2	Mistle thrush 2	Great tit	Bluetit 5
Great tit 2		Bluetit 23	Coal tit
Coal tit 2		Collared dove	Bullfinch M & F
Bluetit 84			Collared dove
Greenfinch 23			Chaffinch
Robin			Robin
Collared dove			Dunnock.
Starling 4			

5th / 6th / 7th

5th	6th	7th
CURRENT 16.5°C	CURRENT 16.5°C	CURRENT 11.5°C
MAX 22°C MIN 11.5°C	MAX 26.5°C MIN 7.5°C	MAX 38.5°C MIN 13.5°C
Greenfinch 26	Collared dove Crow	Crow Collared dove
Great tit 2	Chaffinch (m)	Bluetit
Bluetit	Greenfinch 5	Greenfinch 2
Blackbird	Dunnock	Robin
Dunnock	Starling	Starling
Collared dove	Robin	Blackbird 2
Magpie	Bluetit	Dunnock
Chaffinch (F)	Magpie	Great tit 2

5th / 6th / 7th

5th	6th	Sun. Dec 11 7th
Chaffinch 2	Greenfinch 6	Greenfinch 2
Greenfinch 6	Chaffinch 2	Bluetit 2
Bluetit	Bluetit 2	Dunnock
Coal tit	Coal tit 2	Robin
Great tit	Robin	Coal tit
Blackbird	Collared dove	Chaffinch
Collared dove 2	Greattit	
Jay.	Blackbird	
Dunnock		

Before the drainage of the fenlands some two hundred years ago, the avocet was plentiful. The last breeding colony was destroyed in 1825. After the Second World War a few birds returned to Minsmere and Havergate Island in Suffolk, and began to nest. They now breed every year under protection, in small colonies in Suffolk. Avocets are also regular winter visitors to the Tamar estuary in Devon.

Avocet

SEPTEMBER

YEAR 1	8th	SUN WK. 11	9th		10th		11t
Greenfinch 3 Bluetit 3 Dunnock. Robin		Greenfinch 4/11 Dunnock Bluetit 84 Chaffinch (M)		Collared dove 2		Greenfinch 27 Chaffinch Bluetit 3 Coal tit Collared dove	

YEAR 2 CURRENT 13.5°C	8th MAX 35.5°C MIN 9.5°C	CURRENT 12.5°C	9th MAX 15.5°C MIN 12°C	CURRENT 14°C	10th MAX 37°C MIN 7°C	CURRENT 13°C	11t MAX 35°C MIN 13°C
Great Tit 2 Greenfinch 23 Dunnock Collared dove.		Dunnock Great tit Blackbird Greenfinch 57 Chaffinch Starling Bluetit A. Sparrow Collared dove		COLLARED DOVE Blackbird (M) Dunnock Greenfinch 23 Chaffinch Woodpigeon Starling		Greenfinch 3 Bluetit Chaffinch H. Sparrow Collared dove Chaffinch (M)	

YEAR 3	8th		9th		10th		11t
Greenfinch 85 Coal tit Bluetit Crow Chaffinch 2 Robin Dunnock. Magpie		Dunnock 2 Bluetit 2 Greenfinch 5 Robin Woodpigeon Chaffinch 2 Blackbird Squirrel		Greenfinch 2 Coal tit Collared dove Bluetit Dunnock		Greenfinch 7 Robin Coal tit Blue Tit Great Tit 2 Blackbird Collared dove 2 Chaffinch 2	

SEPTEMBER

	12th		13th		14th
Robin		Collared dove 2			
Greenfinch 7		Bluetit 36			
Bluetit 6		Greenfinch 2940			
Dunnock.		Coal Tit 2			
Coal tit		Great Tit 2			
Collared dove.		Dunnock			
				Harrogate Flower Show.	

CURRENT 16.5°C	12th	CURRENT 15.5°C	13th	CURRENT 16°C	14th
MAX 40·5°C MIN 13°C		MAX 22·5°C MIN 13°C		MAX MIN	
Blackbird (F)		Collared dove 2			
Greenfinch 234		Greenfinch 7			
Bluetit		Blackbird			
Great tit 2		Magpie			
Collared dove 2					
				SCOTLAND	

	12th		13th	SUN. WK 12	14th
Collared dove 23		Greenfinch 5		Greenfinch 36	
Greenfinch 237		Collared dove		Dunnock	
Bluetit				Great tit	
Great tit				Collared dove	
Coal tit				Chaffinch 2	
Chaffinch				Blackbird	
Dunnock 2				Bluetit 2	
Robin .					

ADDITIONAL NOTES:

Arctic skuas can be seen on passage round our coasts at this time of year. Headlands are good places to watch these pirates, as they use their considerable aerial skills to force other sea-birds to give up their catch.

Arctic skua

SEPTEMBER

YEAR 1	15th	Sun. WK. 12.	16th		17th		18th
Greenfinch 3 Bluetit 2 Chaffinch (M) Coal tit ('squirrel!)		Blue tit 3 Dunnock Chaffinch Greenfinch 5 Great tit Collared dove		Greenfinch 45 Bluetit 3 Great tit 23 Dunnock Coal tit Collared dove.		Bluetit 246 Robin Collared dove Dunnock Magpie Greenfinch 4 Great tit 3 Coal tit 2 Chaffinch (M)

YEAR 2	15th		16th		17th		18th

YEAR 3	15th		16th	CURRENT 17°C &	17th		18th
Greenfinch 67 Great tit Collared dove Coal tit Dunnock.		Greenfinch 5 Coal tit 2 Great Tit 1 Bluetit 2 Dunnock 2 Collared dove H. Sparrow Chaffinch		Greenfinch 246 Chaffinch Collared dove 234 Coal tit		Greenfinch 5 Dunnock Bluetit 2 Magpie Chaffinch Robin

SEPTEMBER

	19th	20th	21st
	Bluetit	Bluetit 3	Starling 2
	Great tit	Greenfinch 2	Coal tit
	Coal tit	Coal tit	Bluetit 3
	Greenfinch x 5	Chaffinch (M)	Greenfinch
		Collared dove	Collared dove
		Dunnock	

	19th	20th	21st
			MAX 32°C MIN 7°C
			Starling
			Crow
			Greenfinch 4
			H. Sparrow 3
			Blackbird
			RETURN SCOTLAND

	19th	20th	Sun. Wk 13	21st
	Greenfinch 11	Coal tit	Greenfinch 7	
	Dunnock	Greenfinch 2 5 x 9	Great tit	
	Bluetit 2	Dunnock	Dunnock	
	Collared dove 3	Robin	Collared dove 2	
			Coal tit	

ADDITIONAL NOTES:

As autumn approaches, the seeds of many plants begin to ripen. To take advantage of this harvest, some birds have become specialised feeders. The goldfinch for example, has a fine, sharply pointed bill for extracting seeds from thistles.

Goldfinch

SEPTEMBER

YEAR 1 — 22nd	SUN · WK13 — 23rd	24th	25th
Great Tit 2 Bluetit 4 Dunnock Greenfinch 2+3 Coal tit Chaffinch (F)	Bluetit 2 Robin 1 Blackbird 1 Dunnock Great tit Greenfinch 4 Collared dove 2	Bluetit 3+4 Starling Greenfinch Chaffinch (M)(F) Robin Gr Tit 2 Coal tit Wood pigeon Collared dove.	Collared dove Bluetit 2+3 Greenfinch 2+8 Chaffinch (F) Coal tit Great Tit

YEAR 2 SUN · WK13 CURRENT 14° — 22nd MAX 29.5°C MIN 7.5°C	CURRENT 9°C — 23rd MAX 33°C MIN 6°C	CURRENT 10°C — 24th MAX 33°C MIN 7°C	CURRENT 11·5°C — 25th MAX 24°C MIN 6·5°C
Crow Coal tit Starling Dunnock H.Sparrow 3 Bullfinch (2 Juv.) Greenfinch 8+9+10 Gr tit. Bluetit 2 Blackbird 2 (MF) Collared dove Robin	Collared dove Greenfinch 8+10 Bullfinch (jv) 2 Dunnock Magpie Squirrel	Greenfinch 4+7 Collared dove 3 Starling Coal tit 2 Sparrow H. 2 Blackbird Dunnock Robin Great tit Bluetit	Blackbird Collared dove Chaffinch (F) Greenfinch 2+3 Bluetit (GRANTHAM)

YEAR 3 — 22nd	23rd	24th	25th
Collared dove Greenfinch 4+7 Coal tit Great tit Chaffinch Dunnock	Greenfinch 11 Collared dove Coal tit Chaffinch	Greenfinch 7 Coal tit Great tit Chaffinch Collared dove	Greenfinch 5+10 Bluetit H. Sparrow 3 Collared dove 5+1 Robin.

SEPTEMBER

ADDITIONAL NOTES:

Yr 2. 22nd. 2 Juvenile Bullfinch
1st seen in garden ever!

26th	27th	28th
Bluetit 2	Bluetit 3 5/6	
Greenfinch 3 ♂6	Great Tit ♀3	
Dunnock 2	Greenfinch 5	
Coal tit	Coal tit	
Great tit		
Collared dove		
	Jackies	Jackies

CURRENT 10.5°C 26th	CURRENT 15°C 27th	CURRENT 13.5°C 28th
MAX 20.5°C MIN 10.5°C	MAX ? MIN 12.5°C	MAX 21.5°C MIN 9°C
Greenfinch 2♂6	Blackbird (M)	Collared dove
Coal tit	Greenfinch 2♂♀10	Blackbird 2 (M)
H. Sparrow (H)	Robin Bullfinch 2 (Jv.)	Greenfinch 3
Bluetit	Dunnock	Coal tit 2
Chaffinch	Chaffinch 2 (MF)	Starling 4
Dunnock	Bluetit	
Blackbird (M)	Starling 2	
Starling 3	Collared dove	
	Wren	Helmsley + FA

26th	27th	SUN. OCT. 28th
Greenfinch ♀ 10	Collared dove ♀3	Greenfinch ♀4
Chaffinch 2	Dunnock	Collared dove 2
Collared dove ♀6	Greenfinch 2♀10	Coal tit
Dunnock	Chaffinch	Bluetit 2
Bluetit	Bluetit 3	H. Sparrow ♀3
Robin	Great tit 2	Chaffinch
H. Sparrow 3	Coal tit	Dunnock

A loud tapping noise often reveals the presence of a nuthatch. They feed on acorns, beech mast and hazel nuts, wedging them in the bark of a tree and hammering them open with their pointed bills.

Nuthatch

SEPTEMBER

YEAR 1	29th		30th
~~Wk 1. Sunday~~		Wk 1. Sunday	
~~Collared dove~~		Collared dove	
~~Dunnock~~		~~Blue tit~~	
~~Greenfinch 3♂~~		Dunnock	
Coal tit		Greenfinch	
		Coal tit	
		Janet's	
Jackie's		~~Gale force winds~~ showers	

CURRENT 16°C   CURRENT 16°C

YEAR 2	29th		30th
MAX 27.5°C MIN 8°C		MAX 23°C MIN 10°C	
Cow		Collared dove	
Bullfinch		Bullfinch (jv)	
Greenfinch 25 8 10		Greenfinch 29	
Coal tit 2		Blue tit	
Robin		Robin	
Chaffinch		Chaffinch	
Collared dove			

YEAR 3	29th		30th
Collared dove		Greenfinch 8	
Greenfinch 4 5 7		Blue tit 2	
Dunnock		Dunnock	
Chaffinch 2		Coal tit	
H. Sparrow		H. Sparrow	
Robin		Chaffinch 2	
Blue tit		Collared dove 2	
Great tit			
Coal tit			

SEPTEMBER

The last broods of house martins leave their nests in September. How these young, inexperienced birds find enough time to develop their flying skills before leaving for Africa next month, remains a mystery.

House martins

OCTOBER CHECKLIST

YEAR	1	2	3
DIVERS			
Red-throated diver			
Black-throated diver			
Great Northern diver			
GREBES			
Little grebe			
Great crested grebe			
Red-necked grebe			
Slavonian grebe			
Black-necked grebe			
SHEARWATERS			
Fulmar			
Cory's shearwater			
Great shearwater			
Sooty shearwater			
Manx shearwater			
Mediterranean shearwater			
STORM PETRELS			
Storm petrel			
Leach's petrel			
GANNETS			
Gannet			
CORMORANTS			
Cormorant			
Shag			
HERONS			
Bittern			
Night heron			
Little egret			
Great white egret			
Grey heron			
Purple heron			
IBISES			
Spoonbill			
DUCKS			
Mute swan			
Bewick's swan			
Whooper swan			
Bean goose			
Pink-footed goose			
White-fronted goose			
Greylag goose			
Snow goose			
Canada goose			
Barnacle goose			
Brent goose			
Egyptian goose			
Shelduck			
Mandarin			
Wigeon			
American wigeon			
Gadwall			
Teal			
Mallard			
Pintail			
Garganey			
Shoveler			
Red-crested pochard			

YEAR	1	2	3
DUCKS (cont.)			
Pochard			
Ring-necked duck			
Ferruginous duck			
Tufted duck			
Scaup			
Eider			
King eider			
Long-tailed duck			
Common scoter			
Surf scoter			
Velvet scoter			
Goldeneye			
Smew			
Red-breasted merganser			
Goosander			
Ruddy duck			
HAWKS			
Honey buzzard			
Black kite			
Red kite			
White-tailed eagle			
Marsh harrier			
Hen harrier			
Montagu's harrier			
Goshawk			
Sparrowhawk	✓		
Buzzard			
Rough-legged buzzard			
Golden eagle			
OSPREYS			
Osprey			
FALCONS			
Kestrel			
Red-footed falcon			
Merlin			
Hobby			
Peregrine			
GROUSE			
Red grouse			
Ptarmigan			
Black grouse			
Capercaillie			
PHEASANTS			
Red-legged partridge			
Grey partridge			
Quail			
Pheasant			
Golden pheasant			
Lady Amherst's pheasant			
RAILS			
Water rail			
Spotted crake			
Corncrake			
Moorhen			
Coot			
CRANES			
Crane			

YEAR	1	2	3
OYSTERCATCHERS			
Oystercatcher			
AVOCETS			
Black-winged stilt			
Avocet			
THICK-KNEES			
Stone curlew			
PLOVERS			
Little ringed plover			
Ringed plover			
Kentish plover			
Dotterel			
Golden plover			
Grey plover			
Lapwing			
Turnstone			
SANDPIPERS			
Knot			
Sanderling			
Little stint			
Temminck's stint			
White-rumped sandpiper			
Pectoral sandpiper			
Curlew sandpiper			
Purple sandpiper			
Dunlin			
Buff-breasted sandpiper			
Ruff			
Jack snipe			
Snipe			
Woodcock			
Black-tailed godwit			
Bar-tailed godwit			
Whimbrel			
Curlew			
Spotted redshank			
Redshank			
Marsh sandpiper			
Greenshank			
Green sandpiper			
Wood sandpiper			
Common sandpiper			
PHALAROPES			
Red-necked phalarope			
Grey phalarope			
SKUAS			
Pomarine skua			
Arctic skua			
Long-tailed skua			
Great skua			
GULLS			
Mediterranean gull			
Little gull			
Sabine's gull			
Black-headed gull			
Ring-billed gull			
Common gull			
Lesser black-backed gull			

YEAR	1	2	3
GULLS (cont.)			
Herring gull			
Iceland gull			
Glaucous gull			
Great black-backed gull			
Kittiwake			
Sandwich tern			
Roseate tern			
Common tern			
Arctic tern			
Little tern			
Black tern			
White-winged black tern			
AUKS			
Guillemot			
Razorbill			
Black guillemot			
Little auk			
Puffin			
PIGEONS			
Rock dove			
Stock dove			
Wood-pigeon	✓		✓
Collared dove	✓	✓	✓
Turtle dove			
PARROTS			
Ring-necked parakeet			
CUCKOOS			
Cuckoo			
BARN OWLS			
Barn owl			
OWLS			
Snowy owl			
Little owl			
Tawny owl			
Long-eared owl			
Short-eared owl			
NIGHTJARS			
Nightjar			
SWIFTS			
Swift			
Alpine swift			
KINGFISHERS			
Kingfisher			
BEE-EATERS			
Bee-eater			
HOOPOES			
Hoopoe			
WOODPECKERS			
Wryneck			
Green woodpecker			
Great spotted woodpecker.			
Lesser spotted woodpecker.			
LARKS			
Short-toed lark			
Woodlark			
Skylark			
Shore lark			

YEAR	1	2
SWALLOWS		
Sand martin		
Swallow		
House martin		
PIPITS		
Richard's pipit		
Tawny pipit		
Tree pipit		
Meadow pipit		
Red-throated pipit		
Rock pipit		
Water pipit		
Yellow wagtail		
Grey wagtail		
Pied wagtail		
WAXWINGS		
Waxwing		
DIPPERS		
Dipper		
WRENS		
Wren		
ACCENTORS		
Dunnock	✓	✓
THRUSHES		
Robin	✓	✓
Nightingale		
Bluethroat		
Black redstart		
Redstart		
Whinchat		
Stonechat		
Wheatear		
Ring ouzel		
Blackbird	✓	✓
Fieldfare		
Song thrush		
Redwing		
Mistle thrush	✓	✓
FLYCATCHERS		
Cetti's warbler		
Grasshopper warbler		
Savi's warbler		
Aquatic warbler		
Sedge warbler		
Marsh warbler		
Reed warbler		
Icterine warbler		
Melodious warbler		
Dartford warbler		
Subalpine warbler		
Barred warbler		
Lesser whitethroat		
Whitethroat		
Garden warbler		
Blackcap		
Pallas's warbler		
Yellow-browed warbler		
Wood warbler		

NON-LISTED SIGHTINGS

Bullfinches are thought to pair for life, the male and female birds being seen together throughout the year. This is unusual behaviour, as most finches form mixed flocks outside of the breeding season.

OCTOBER

YEAR 1	1st	2nd	3rd	4t
Collared dove Bluetit	Bluetit		Coal tit 2 Bluetit 2 Greenfinch Great tit 2	
Galeforce winds / showers	Strong winds – Nth Sea Lerries	Holland.	Nth Sea Lerries 7. A.	

YEAR 2 CURRENT 15.5°C	1st CURRENT 14.5°C	2nd CURRENT 14°C	3rd CURRENT 11.5°C	4t
MAX 25.5°C MIN 12°C	MAX 24°C MIN 10°C	MAX 24.5°C MIN 6.5°C	MAX 30°C MIN 11°C	
Coal tit 3 Chaffinch Bullfinch (2jv) Greenfinch 5 Collared dove 2 Carrion Crow Bluetit Wren	Greenfinch 15 Bluetit 10 Coal tit Great Tit 2 Long tailed tit 2 Rook Collared dove 2 H. Sparrow	Greenfinch 39 Collared dove 2 Bluetit Rook	Robin H Sparrow Dunnock 2 Chaffinch Collared dove 3 Blackbird M Greenfinch 16 Coal tit Bluetit 24 Great tit 2 Starling (windy)	

YEAR 3	1st	2nd	3rd	4t
Collared dove Chaffinch 2 Greenfinch 2 Dunnock Coal tit Bluetit 2	Collared dove 3 Greenfinch 46 Dunnock Chaffinch H. Sparrow Bluetit Robin	Collared dove 2 Bluetit Chaffinch Greenfinch 26 Coal tit 2 Dunnock.	Robin Dunnock Greenfinch 7 Coal tit Collared dove H. Sparrow	

ADDITIONAL NOTES:
2002 2nd Oct. Flock of all 4 type
of tit wheeling- flying round over 20
in all. v. briefly about 5 mins
2003 7th Oct Jay in tree

5th

Greenfinch
Collared dove

Rain.

6th

Bluetits 2
Great tit 2
Greenfinch 2

Wk2 Sun. **7th**

Bluetit 2
Magpie 2
Coal tit 2
Greenfinch
Collared dove 2
Robin
Wood pigeon
Great tit 2

CURRENT 15°C **5th**
MAX 24°C MIN 8°C
Greenfinch ♂♀8
Collared dove
- Sparrow (M)
Bluetit
Coal tit
Dunnock

SUN. WK2. CURRENT 13°C **6th**
MAX 31.5°C MIN 10°C
Greenfinch ♂♀10
Coal Tit
Bluetit
Starling 3
Blackbird (M)
Chaffinch (F) 2
H. Sparrow (M) 2
Dunnock
Collared dove 2

CURRENT 12°C **7th**
MAX 30°C MIN 10°C
Robin
Greenfinch 3
Collared dove
Starling
Great tit
Bluetit

SUN WK2. **5th**
Collared dove 2
Coal tit ♀3
Greenfinch ♂♀8
Dunnock 2
Magpie 2
Chaffinch
Great tit 2
Bluetit

6th
Greenfinch 3
Collared dove 3
Dunnock
Robin
Magpie

7th
Greenfinch 5 6
Collared dove 5 6
Dunnock
Chaffinch
Robin
Albino Wood pigeon.
Jay

Hen harriers are present all year; during the summer months they are mostly seen on their moorland breeding grounds. In October, however, the birds become widespread, giving more of us an opportunity to observe them.

Hen harrier

OCTOBER

YEAR 1	8th	9th	10th	11th
Blue tit Great tit 2 Collared dove Blackbird Greenfinch Magpie Sparrowhawk		Scarborough	Great tit 2 Sparrowhawk	Blue tit Great tit Coal tit Robin

YEAR 2 CURRENT 10.5°C 8th MAX 20.5°C MIN 5°C	CURRENT 10°C 9th MAX 16°C MIN 7.5°C	CURRENT 13.5°C 10th MAX 16.5°C MIN 10°C	CURRENT 12°C 11th MAX 16.5°C MIN 8.5°C
Greenfinch 6 Starling 3 Blue tit H. Sparrow Collared dove 2	Starling Greenfinch 26 Collared dove	Collared dove Greenfinch 49 Blue tit Coal tit 2 H. Sparrow Dunnock Chaffinch (F) Blackbird (M)	Greenfinch 30 Dunnock 2 Wren Starling 2 Collared dove 2 Coal tit 2 H. Sparrow Blue tit 3 Long tailed tit
(FA)	FA		

YEAR 3	8th	9th	10th	11th
Collared dove 2 Greenfinch 48 Chaffinch Dunnock Robin Blue tit Coal tit 2 Great tit	Collared dove 4 Greenfinch 7 Blue tit 2 Great tit Jay Chaffinch Coal tit Dunnock Blackbird	Collared dove 5 Greenfinch 4 Blue tit Jay Magpie 2 Crow 2	Collared dove 2 Blue tit Dunnock Blackbird Greenfinch 6 H. Sparrow Chaffinch Jay

OCTOBER

12th

Robin
Bluetit 2
Coal tit 2
Greenfinch
Great tit

13th

Dunnock (nearly caught by cat on birdtable)
Bluetit 2
Greenfinch
Robin
Coal tit
Sparrowhawk.

14th — Sun. lok 3.

Great tit 2
Coal tit 2
Bluetit 2
Collared dove
Jay

12th
CURRENT 9.5°C
MAX 13°C MIN 2.5°C
Greenfinch 7

Helmsley & FA

13th — SUN WKS
CURRENT 5°C
MAX 15°C MIN 4.5°C
Greenfinch   Bullfinch 2
Coal tit
Collared dove
H. Sparrow
Starling 5
Dunnock
Chaffinch (F)
Blackbird
Bluetit 2

14th
CURRENT 9°C
MAX 13°C MIN 5.5°C
Collared dove
Greenfinch 87
Bluetit

12th — SUN LOK 3.

Collared dove   Crow
Dunnock   Robin
Coal tit
Great tit
Bluetit
Greenfinch
Blackbird
Chaffinch
H. Sparrow

13th — Sun. lok 3.

Collared dove 23
H. Sparrow 3
Chaffinch 2
Greenfinch 8
Blackbird

14th

Collared dove 23
Bluetit 3   Chaffinch
Blackbird 4
Dunnock
Greenfinch 45
Robin
Starling
Great tit 3
Coal tit 2

ADDITIONAL NOTES:

2001
Sparrowhawk again on 8th. Think I saw it flying 2 wks earlier. Jay on 14th. Only 3rd time in 16 yrs.

2003. 9th Oct. Jay at bird table. 8th time in 16 yrs! 10th Jay in tree

Most common scoters are winter visitors, forming large 'rafts' around Britain's coasts. They return from their Arctic breeding grounds in September, remaining with us until April.

Common scoter

OCTOBER

YEAR 1 15th	16th	17th	18th
Great tit	Bluetit 2	Bluetit 2	Woodpigeon
Coal tit	Coal tit 2	Coal tit 2	Bluetit 2
Mistle Thrush	Collared dove.	Great tit 23	
Dunnock		Greenfinch	
Blackbird			
Magpie			
Bullfinch (M)			

YEAR 2 CURRENT 6.5°C 15th MAX 11.5°C MIN 4.5°C	CURRENT 6.5°C 16th MAX 13.5°C MIN 2.5°C	CURRENT 5°C 17th MAX 11°C MIN 1.5°C	CURRENT 2.5°C 18th COULDN'T GET READINGS MAX MIN BOTHER!
Greenfinch 12	Greenfinch 8	Coal tit	Greenfinch 9
Chaffinch (F) 2	H. Sparrow	Greenfinch 6	Bullfinch 2
Great tit	Coal tit	Starlings 2	Collared dove
H. Sparrow	Collared dove	Blackbird 8	Blackbird 23
Coal tit	Bluetit	Robin	Coal tit 2
Starling 3	Blackbird	Chaffinch	Bluetit
Bluetit	Dunnock	Collared dove	Magpie

YEAR 3 15th	16th	17th	18th
Robin	Collared dove 3	Collared dove 3	Bluetit
Woodpigeon	Starling 2	Bluetit	Collared dove 2
	Greenfinch 9	Coal tit	Greenfinch 5
	Bluetit	Great tit 2	Blackbird
	Coal tit	Greenfinch 4	Chaffinch
	Great tit	Starling	Coal tit
		Chaffinch 2	Dunnock
St. James Hosp		Dunnock	Squirrel
Peter & Janet.			

OCTOBER

21st 2002 2 wrens in nesting box by upstairs patio-doors!!

	19th		20th	10k 4 Sun.	21st
Blue tit		Blue tit 2		2 Bluetits	
Coal tit 2		Great tit		Collared dove	
Great tit x3		Robin			
Dunnock		Coal tit x3			
		Blackbird (F)			

CURRENT 0.5°C	19th	CURRENT 1°C SUNNY	20th	CURRENT 8°C	21st
MAX 17.5°C MIN 0°C		MAX 10°C MIN 1°C			
Blue tit		Starling 2		Blue tit	
Greenfinch x8		Greenfinch 3		Coal tit	
Coal tit		Blue tit		Wren	
Blackbird		H. Sparrow		Greenfinch x3	
Collared dove		Chaffinch		Blackbird (M)	
		Dunnock		Magpie	
		Coal tit		H. Sparrow	

Sun. 10k 4	19th		20th		21st
Coal tit		Magpie 2		Collared dove 3	
Collared dove		Blue tit		Blue tit 2	
Greenfinch 3		Robin		Greenfinch 5	
Chaffinch 2 (F)		Greenfinch 2		Coal tit 2	
Robin		H. Sparrow		Wren	
Blue tit		Coal tit		Chaffinch	
Magpie 2				Dunnock	Cat
Wren					

Oak-woods in October provide abundant crops of acorns, a source of food exploited by many birds and mammals. Jays in particular, love them, eating their fill and burying others in larders for winter when food is scarce.

Jay

OCTOBER

YEAR 1	22nd	23rd	24th	25th
Bluetit 2 Coal tit 2 Woodpigeon		Coal tit ×2 Bluetit ×2 Blackbird Gt. Tit		
		Brimham	Brimham	Brimham

YEAR 2	22nd	23rd	24th	25th
				MAX 20°C MIN 0·5°C Greenfinch 4

YEAR 3	22nd	23rd	24th	25th
Greenfinch 8+7 Bluetit 2,3 Great tit Coal tit Chaffinch H. Sparrow Crow		Collared dove Greenfinch 2,6 Bluetit 2 Coal tit Great tit Chaffinch 2 Dunnock Blackbird	Blackbird Collared dove 2 Bluetit Greenfinch 4 Dunnock	Song thrush Jay Blackbird Robin Collared dove H. Sparrow Greenfinch 2,10 Bluetit 2,5 Great tit 2 Coal tit Long tailed tit 5 Chaffinch

OCTOBER

ADDITIONAL NOTES:
2003 25th 5 long tailed tits among mixed flock of all the tits. Brilliant day for birds!!
2003 26th 2 Jays never before! 27th too After peanuts. Magpie attacked them.
2003 28th Redwing 1st the season.

	26th		27th	Sun. Wk 5		28th
				Blackbird 2		
				Greenfinch 2		
				Coal tit 23		
				Bluetit 2		
				Robin		

Brimham

Brimham

CURRENT. 6°C	26th	SUN WK5 CURRENT 11°C	27th	CURRENT 5.5°C	28th
MAX 20.5°C MIN 5.5°C		MAX 13°C MIN 3°C		MAX 12.5°C MIN 5.5°C	
Greenfinch 8 & 10		Greenfinch 7 9		Collared dove 2	
Bluetit 2		Collared dove		Greenfinch 3	
Coal tit		Blackbird (M) 3		Dunnock	
Chaffinch (F)		H. Sparrow (M)			
Dunnock		Coal tit			
Crow		Bluetit			
Blackbird (M)		Chaffinch (F)			
		GTALES • RAIN			

WK 5 SUN	26th	MIN ? 2°C MAX 11°C?	27th	CURRENT 10°C	28th
CURRENT TEMP 5.5°C		CURRENT 7°C		MAX 11°C MIN 6°C	
Jay 2		Blackbird 2 Coal tit		Blackbird 2 Great tit 2	
Chaffinch 2		Great tit Collared dove 2		Bluetit Crow	
Greenfinch 3		Greenfinch 4 Jay 2		Chaffinch 2 Coal tit	
Magpie		Chaffinch		Greenfinch 5	
Great tit 2		Dunnock		Magpie	
Bluetit		H. Sparrow 3		H. Sparrow	
Song Thrush.		Bluetit		Redwing	
Blackbird. Squirrel		Robin Cat		Dunnock	
		Mistle Thrush Song		Collared dove 2	

Huge numbers of waterfowl arrive in Britain every autumn to overwinter. Greylag geese from Iceland join our resident greylags in October. They pair for life, reinforcing their bond with a noisy 'triumph ceremony' each time they meet.

Greylag geese

OCTOBER

Much milder than usual. No leaves off trees yet. Bird nos. low.

YEAR 1 29th	30th	31st
Great tit	Blackbirds 5 Carrion Crow 2	Collared dove Blackbird Coal tit Greenfinch Gt. Tit.
High winds	V. High winds	Highish winds

YEAR 2 CURRENT 6.5°C 29th MAX 9°C MIN 3°C	CURRENT 5°C 30th MAX 15.5°C MIN 3°C	CURRENT 9.5°C 31st MAX 15°C MIN 9°C
Greenfinch +b 24	Collared dove	Bluetit 2
Starling 2	Great tit	Great tit
Coal tit	Greenfinch +6	Greenfinch +10
Blackbird 3	Starling 3	Starling
Collared dove 34	Blackbird b3	Robin
Mistle Thrush	Bluetit	Blackbird
Bluetit 2	Coal tit 2	
Dunnock	Wren	
Chaffinch	(Heron fly)	

YEAR 3 29th	MAX 10°C 30th CURRENT 7.5°C	31st
Blackbird 5	Blackbird Great tit	Blackbird 5 H. Sparrow 3
Collared dove 3	Robin Crow	Collared dove 24 Bluetit
Jay 2	Greenfinch 26	Great tit 2
Great tit	Coal tit	Greenfinch 45
Greenfinch 5	H. Sparrow 2	Coal tit
H. Sparrow	Chaffinch 1	Dunnock
Coal tit 2	Dunnock	Jay
Chaffinch	Jay 2	Chaffinch 2
Bluetit	Collared dove	Robin

OCTOBER

Short-eared owls often hunt in daylight, flying low over open countryside. In autumn and winter they become much more widespread, often appearing in areas outside of their breeding grounds.

Short-eared owl

NOVEMBER CHECKLIST

YEAR	1	2	3
DIVERS			
Red-throated diver			
Black-throated diver			
Great Northern diver			
GREBES			
Little grebe			
Great crested grebe			
Red-necked grebe			
Slavonian grebe			
Black-necked grebe			
SHEARWATERS			
Fulmar			
Cory's shearwater			
Great shearwater			
Sooty shearwater			
Manx shearwater			
Mediterranean shearwater			
STORM PETRELS			
Storm petrel			
Leach's petrel			
GANNETS			
Gannet			
CORMORANTS			
Cormorant			
Shag			
HERONS			
Bittern			
Night heron			
Little egret			
Great white egret			
Grey heron			
Purple heron			
IBISES			
Spoonbill			
DUCKS			
Mute swan			
Bewick's swan			
Whooper swan			
Bean goose			
Pink-footed goose			
White-fronted goose			
Greylag goose			
Snow goose			
Canada goose			
Barnacle goose			
Brent goose			
Egyptian goose			
Shelduck			
Mandarin			
Wigeon			
American wigeon			
Gadwall			
Teal			
Mallard			
Pintail			
Garganey			
Shoveler			
Red-crested pochard			

YEAR	1	2	3
DUCKS (cont.)			
Pochard			
Ring-necked duck			
Ferruginous duck			
Tufted duck			
Scaup			
Eider			
King eider			
Long-tailed duck			
Common scoter			
Surf scoter			
Velvet scoter			
Goldeneye			
Smew			
Red-breasted merganser			
Goosander			
Ruddy duck			
HAWKS			
Honey buzzard			
Black kite			
Red kite			
White-tailed eagle			
Marsh harrier			
Hen harrier			
Montagu's harrier			
Goshawk			
Sparrowhawk			
Buzzard			
Rough-legged buzzard			
Golden eagle			
OSPREYS			
Osprey			
FALCONS			
Kestrel			
Red-footed falcon			
Merlin			
Hobby			
Peregrine			
GROUSE			
Red grouse			
Ptarmigan			
Black grouse			
Capercaillie			
PHEASANTS			
Red-legged partridge			
Grey partridge			
Quail			
Pheasant			
Golden pheasant			
Lady Amherst's pheasant			
RAILS			
Water rail			
Spotted crake			
Corncrake			
Moorhen			
Coot			
CRANES			
Crane			

YEAR	1	2	3
OYSTERCATCHERS			
Oystercatcher			
AVOCETS			
Black-winged stilt			
Avocet			
THICK-KNEES			
Stone curlew			
PLOVERS			
Little ringed plover			
Ringed plover			
Kentish plover			
Dotterel			
Golden plover			
Grey plover			
Lapwing			
Turnstone			
SANDPIPERS			
Knot			
Sanderling			
Little stint			
Temminck's stint			
White-rumped sandpiper			
Pectoral sandpiper			
Curlew sandpiper			
Purple sandpiper			
Dunlin			
Buff-breasted sandpiper			
Ruff			
Jack snipe			
Snipe			
Woodcock			
Black-tailed godwit			
Bar-tailed godwit			
Whimbrel			
Curlew			
Spotted redshank			
Redshank			
Marsh sandpiper			
Greenshank			
Green sandpiper			
Wood sandpiper			
Common sandpiper			
PHALAROPES			
Red-necked phalarope			
Grey phalarope			
SKUAS			
Pomarine skua			
Arctic skua			
Long-tailed skua			
Great skua			
GULLS			
Mediterranean gull			
Little gull			
Sabine's gull			
Black-headed gull			
Ring-billed gull			
Common gull			
Lesser black-backed gull			

YEAR	1	2	3
GULLS (cont.)			
Herring gull			
Iceland gull			
Glaucous gull			
Great black-backed gull			
Kittiwake			
Sandwich tern			
Roseate tern			
Common tern			
Arctic tern			
Little tern			
Black tern			
White-winged black tern			
AUKS			
Guillemot			
Razorbill			
Black guillemot			
Little auk			
Puffin			
PIGEONS			
Rock dove			
Stock dove			
Wood-pigeon			
Collared dove	✔	✔	
Turtle dove			
PARROTS			
Ring-necked parakeet			
CUCKOOS			
Cuckoo			
BARN OWLS			
Barn owl			
OWLS			
Snowy owl			
Little owl			
Tawny owl			
Long-eared owl			
Short-eared owl			
NIGHTJARS			
Nightjar			
SWIFTS			
Swift			
Alpine swift			
KINGFISHERS			
Kingfisher			
BEE-EATERS			
Bee-eater			
HOOPOES			
Hoopoe			
WOODPECKERS			
Wryneck			
Green woodpecker			
Great spotted woodpecker.			
Lesser spotted woodpecker			
LARKS			
Short-toed lark			
Woodlark			
Skylark			
Shore lark			

YEAR	1	2
SWALLOWS		
Sand martin		
Swallow		
House martin		
PIPITS		
Richard's pipit		
Tawny pipit		
Tree pipit		
Meadow pipit		
Red-throated pipit		
Rock pipit		
Water pipit		
Yellow wagtail		
Grey wagtail		
Pied wagtail		
WAXWINGS		
Waxwing		
DIPPERS		
Dipper		
WRENS		
Wren		
ACCENTORS		
Dunnock	✔	✔
THRUSHES		
Robin	✔	✔
Nightingale		
Bluethroat		
Black redstart		
Redstart		
Whinchat		
Stonechat		
Wheatear		
Ring ouzel		
Blackbird	✔	✔
Fieldfare		
Song thrush		
Redwing		
Mistle thrush		
FLYCATCHERS		
Cetti's warbler		
Grasshopper warbler		
Savi's warbler		
Aquatic warbler		
Sedge warbler		
Marsh warbler		
Reed warbler		
Icterine warbler		
Melodious warbler		
Dartford warbler		
Subalpine warbler		
Barred warbler		
Lesser whitethroat		
Whitethroat		
Garden warbler		
Blackcap		
Pallas's warbler		
Yellow-browed warbler		
Wood warbler		

YEAR	1	2	3
[FL]YCATCHERS (cont.)			
[C]hiffchaff			
[W]illow warbler			
[G]oldcrest		✓	
[Fi]recrest			
[Sp]otted flycatcher			
[R]ed-breasted flycatcher			
[Pi]ed flycatcher			
[R]EEDLINGS			
[Be]arded tit			
[TI]TMICE			
[Lo]ng-tailed tit			
[M]arsh tit			
[W]illow tit			
[Cr]ested tit			
[Co]al tit	✓	✓	
[Blu]e tit	✓	✓	
[Gr]eat tit	✓	✓	
[N]UTHATCHES			
[Nu]thatch			
[C]REEPERS			
[Tr]eecreeper			
[O]RIOLES			
[Go]lden oriole			
[S]HRIKES			
[Red]-backed shrike			
[Gr]eat Grey shrike			
[Wo]odchat shrike			
[C]ROWS			
[Ja]y			
[M]agpie	✓		
[C]hough			
[Ja]ckdaw			
[Ro]ok			
[Ca]rrion crow	✓	✓	
[Ra]ven			
[ST]ARLINGS			
[St]arling			
[S]PARROWS			
[Ho]use sparrow		✓	
[Tr]ee sparrow			
[B]UNTINGS			
[La]pland bunting			
[Sn]ow bunting			
[Ye]llowhammer			
[Ci]rl bunting			
[Or]tolan bunting			
[Li]ttle bunting			
[Re]ed bunting			
[Co]rn bunting			
[FI]NCHES			
[Ch]affinch	✓	✓	
[Bra]mbling			
[Se]rin			
[Gr]eenfinch	✓	✓	
[Go]ldfinch			
[Si]skin			
[Li]nnet			

YEAR	1	2	3
FINCHES (cont.)			
Twite			
Redpoll			
Arctic redpoll			
Crossbill			
Scottish crossbill			
Scarlet rosefinch			
Bullfinch			
Hawfinch			

NON-LISTED SIGHTINGS

The redwing is an attractive member of the thrush family and is mostly a winter visitor to Britain. Its breeding range is increasing, with some birds now regularly nesting in northern Scotland.

NOVEMBER

YEAR 1 1st	2nd	3rd	4th
Blackbird 2 3	Blackbirds 10	Coal tits 2	Sun Wk 6. Blackbird 2
Mistle Thrush	Great tit	Great tit	Greenfinch
Greenfinch	Bluetit	Dunnock	Coal tit
Bluetit 4		Bluetit 3	Magpie
Great tit 2			Bluetit
Coal tit			
Chaffinch (M)			
	Helmsley		

2002 YEAR 2 CURRENT 11·5°C 1st	CURRENT 10°C 2nd	CURRENT 11°C Wk6 Sun 3rd	CURRENT 8°C 4th
MAX 16·5°C MIN 8·5°C	MAX 15°C MIN 6·5°C	MAX 20·5°C MIN 6°C	MAX 20°C MIN 5·5°C
Blackbird 6	Collared dove 2	Starling 4	Robin
Starling 3	Bluetit 2	Greenfinch 10	Bluetit
Greenfinch 8 10	Greenfinch 2	Dunnock 2	Coal tit
Collared dove 2	Bullfinch (Imm)	Chaffinch (F)(M)	Blackbird 2 3
Bluetit 2	Starling 2	Bluetit	Greenfinch 4
Dunnock	Blackbird 2	Collared dove 4	GOLDCREST
	Dunnock	Blackbird	Collared dove 3
	Great tit	Robin	Chaffinch (F M) 2
		H. Sparrow	Starling

YEAR 3 MAX 11·5°C 1st CURRENT 6°C 8.30am	SUN Wk6 CURRENT 13·5°C (9.15am) 2nd	CURRENT 10°C (9.31am) 3rd	4th
Crow 2 H. Sparrow 2	Jay	Collared dove 2 3	Greenfinch 3 Blackbird
Jay Great tit	Collared dove 4	Greenfinch 5 7	Dunnock
Blackbird 3 4 Dunnock	Magpie 2	Chaffinch 2 Dunnock	Bullfinch
Bluetit	Greenfinch 4	Bluetit Coal tit	Starling 2
Coal tit	Bluetit 2 3	Great tit	H. Sparrow
Robin	Great tit 2	Crow	Chaffinch 2
Greenfinch 5	Coal tit 2	Magpie	Bluetit 2
Chaffinch	Chaffinch 2	Blackbird	Coal tit
Song thrush	Blackbird	H. Sparrow 3	Jay

NOVEMBER

ADDITIONAL NOTES: 2002 4th Nov GOLDCREST 1st Time ever!
2003 6th Nov. " 2nd " " !

	5th	6th	7th
Coal tit 3	Great tit 2	Blackbird 3
Blue tit	Coal tit	Coal tit 2
Dunnock		Blue tit
Great tit		
Blackbird 2		
Robin		
Greenfinch		
	Fountains Abbey	Fountains Abbey

	5th	6th	7th
CURRENT 11.5°C max 15.5°C MIN 10.5°C	CURRENT 11°C MAX 14.5°C MIN 4°C	CURRENT 7°C MAX — MIN 4.5°C
Collared dove 3	Collared dove	Greenfinch 3
Greenfinch 3	Blackbird	
Blackbird 2	Greenfinch 6	
Coal tit 2	Blue tit	
	Robin	
	Crow	
	Dunnock	
Helmsley & Beadlam.		(Just no birds!)

	5th	6th	7th CURRENT 11°C
Greenfinch 234	Jay	Jay 2
Blackbird	Greenfinch 6	Blue tit 2
Jay	Chaffinch 2	Blackbird 2
Dunnock 2	Blackbird 23	Greenfinch 24
Blue tit 2	Goldcrest	Chaffinch 2
Sparrow 3	Collared dove 2	Great tit
Collared dove 34	Magpie	Coal tit
Chaffinch 23	Blue tit 2	Squirrel
Great tit	Dunnock	

Large flocks of fieldfares are a common sight, feeding in fields or on roadside hawthorn berries in winter. They are rather noisy birds with distinctive chattering calls which are often heard as they fly overhead.

Fieldfare

NOVEMBER

YEAR 1 8th	9th	10th	11t
Blue tit 2	Chaffinch (M+F) 2	Coal tit	Sun. Wk 7
Greenfinch	Blue tit 2&3	Blackbird	
Blackbird 2	Coal tit 2		
Robin	Blackbird 2		
Carrion Crow	Great tit 2		
Coal tit	Dunnock		
Magpie 3			
Snow showers Bitterly cold		Northumberland	Northumberland

YEAR 2 CURRENT 8·5° 8th	CURRENT 7·5°C 9th	SUN WK7. CURRENT 9°C 10th	CURRENT 9·5°C 11t
MAX 10·5°C MIN 4·5°C	MAX 14·5°C MIN 3·5°C	MAX 14·5°C MIN 3·5°C	MAX 12·5°C MIN 4°C
Blackbird 2&3	Blackbird 4	Greenfinch ?10&12 Crow	Collared dove 2
Greenfinch ?9	Greenfinch ?8&10	Blackbird 3 H. Sparrow	Blackbird 2
Robin	Collared dove 3	Collared dove 3 Chaffinch F&M	Great tit
Blue tit	Blue tit	Starling 2&3 Blue tit 3	Blue tit 2
Dunnock	Coal tit	Great tit 2	Greenfinch 6
Collared dove	Chaffinch (F)	Robin	
	Robin	Coal tit	
	H. Sparrow	Dunnock	
Helmsley & Beadlam		Magpie	

YEAR 3 8th	CURRENT 12°C (9.45am) 9th SUN WK7	10th	11t
Collared dove 4 Crow	Crow Coal tit	Blackbird	Greenfinch ?8&10
Dunnock	Collared dove	Dunnock 2	Blackbird 2
Great tit 2	Blackbird 2	Greenfinch 2&4	Collared dove 2
Greenfinch ?10	Greenfinch 2	Blue tit 2	Blue tit 2
Chaffinch 3	Great tit	Great tit 2	Great tit
Coal tit	Blue tit	Chaffinch 3	Chaffinch 2
Blackbird	Dunnock	H. Sparrow 2	Jay
Blue tit 2	Jay 2	Jay	Goldfinch 3
Jay	Chaffinch	Robin	Dunnock

NOVEMBER

12th	13th	14th
neat tit		Coal tit
bluetit 2		
coal tit		
Robin		
	Fountains Abbey	Fountains Abbey

12th	13th	14th
CURRENT 7°C MAX 12°C MIN 3.5°C	CURRENT 4.5°C MAX 13°C MIN 4°C	CURRENT 11°C MAX 12°C MIN 3°C
Blackbird 2	Robin	Greenfinch 810
Greenfinch 2	Greenfinch 8+8	Robin
coal tit	Dunnock	Blackbird 2
Great tit 2	Bluetit	Collared dove
Starling 7		Coal tit
bluetit 2		Bluetit 3
long tailed tit		Chaffinch (F)
Robin		
	(Helmsley)	

12th	13th	14th
Greenfinch	Greenfinch	Collared dove 83
blackbird	Bluetit 2	Jay
Collared dove 3	Collared dove 2	Greenfinch 84680011
Jay 2	Jay	Bluetit 2
	Dunnock	Chaffinch 2
		Dunnock
		Blackbird
		Coal tit
Danley Mills		Great tit

ADDITIONAL NOTES:

Razorbills are members of the auk family, they can be seen around our coasts all year. The distinctive bill is, perhaps not surprisingly, very sharp. It is used to deal with the fish, crustaceans and shellfish that make up the bird's diet.

Razorbill

NOVEMBER

YEAR 1 15th	16th	17th	Sun. Wk8 18t
Blackbird 2 Robin Dunnock Collared dove	Coal tit 2 Bluetit 23 Blackbird Chaffinch	Coal tit 2 Chaffinch 2 (M&F) Bluetit Robin Blackbird (M)(F) Great tit 2	Blackbirds 3 Bluetit 2 Great tit 2 Robin Coal tit 2 Chaffinch (F) Dunnock To Grasmere

YEAR 2 CURRENT 6·5°C 15th	16th	SUN Wk8 17th	CURRENT 3°C 18t
MAX MIN Starling 27 Collared dove 3 Greenfinch 25 Robin		MAX 15°C MIN 2°C	MAX 10°C MIN 2·5°C Collared dove Greenfinch 23
Helmsley	Helmsley (Dad died)	Helmsley	Helmsley (day only)

YEAR 3 15th	SUN Wk8 16th	17th	18t
CURRENT 8°C Collared dove 2 Jay Blue tit Great tit Greenfinch 29 Chaffinch 2 Coal tit Dunnock Blackbird	CURRENT 3°C Chaffinch 3 Crow Greenfinch 4 Robin Great tit 2 Coal tit Jay Blackbird Dunnock Bluetit Collared dove 2	Greenfinch 39 Coal tit Jay Chaffinch 23 Bluetit 2 Collared dove 2 Great tit Blackbird	CURRENT 10°C Collared dove 24 Chaffinch 34 Bluetit Greenfinch 26 Coal tit Great tit 2 Jay Starling 85 Woodpigeon Squirrel Blackbird 2

NOVEMBER

	19th		20th		21st

Grasmere	19th	Grasmere	20th	Grasmere	21st
CURRENT 4.5°C		CURRENT 8.5°C		CURRENT 11°C	
MAX 12°C MIN 3.5°C		MAX 12°C MIN 6.5°C		MAX 14.5°C MIN 6.5°C	
Collared dove 4 5		Collared dove 2		Collared dove 8 7 9	
Starling 5				Starling 2	
Blackbird 2				Great tit 3	
Bluetit 2				Greenfinch 8 10	
Dunnock 2				Bluetit 2	
Greenfinch 4				Magpie	
H-Sparrow				Chaffinch (1)	
Robin		Helmsley (day only)			

	19th		20th		21st
CURRENT 8°C		CURRENT 8°C		CURRENT 4°C	
Jay		Jay		Chaffinch	
Collared dove 2		Collared dove		Jay	
Greenfinch 3 4 6		Greenfinch 24		Bluetit 2	
Dunnock		Chaffinch		Great tit 2	
		Great tit			
		Blackbird			

ADDITIONAL NOTES:

Estuary mud is full of food for hungry wading birds. Redshanks move to the coast after the breeding season, to take their share of this rich harvest. The birds feed largely by sight, picking up small invertebrates from the surface of the mud.

Redshank

NOVEMBER

YEAR 1	22nd		23rd		24th	Sun Wk 9.	25t
				Dunnock		Blackbird	
				Bluetit		Coal tit	
						Bluetit	
						Robin	
						Dunnock	
						Greenfinch	
Grasmere		Grasmere		Return Grasmere			

YEAR 2	CURRENT 12°C	22nd	CURRENT 7.5°C	23rd	Sun Wk 9 CURRENT 6°C	24th	CURRENT 4°C	25t
MAX 13.5°C MIN 4°		MAX 11.5°C MIN 4°C		MAX 1°C MIN 2°C		MAX MIN	
Collared dove 23		Collared dove 5		Collared dove		Bluetit 2	
Greenfinch 3		Greenfinch 5 10.11.14		Chaffinch (M)(F) 2		Robin	
		Starling 8		Starling 2		Blackbird	
		Bluetit		Blackbird 2			
		Blackbird		Greenfinch 4 34			
		Chaffinch (M)		Coal tit 2 Coal tit			
		Dunnock		Robin			
				Do			
Helmsley (Funeral)				Grasmere		Grasmere	

YEAR 3	22nd	Sunday Wk 9	23rd		24th		25t
CURRENT 3°C		CURRENT 0°C					
Collared dove 2		Collared dove 2 Robin		Jay 2.			
Bluetit		Starling 4 6 H. Sparrow		Dunnock			
Coal tit		Bluetit 2					
		Jay					
		Greenfinch 23					
		Coal tit					
		Chaffinch 2 34					
		Dunnock					
Mansfield - Ursula		Great tit 1		GRASMERE		Grasmere	

NOVEMBER

	26th	27th	28th
Bluetit 2	Dunnock	
Blackbird	Collared dove	
Chaffinch (F)	Coal tit	
Robin	Great tit 2	
Dunnock	Bluetit	
		Anns Hebden

	26th	27th	28th
Grasmere	Grasmere	Grasmere

	26th	27th	28th
Grasmere	Grasmere	Grasmere

ADDITIONAL NOTES:

Wigeon form large flocks on salt marshes and mudflats in winter. These attractive ducks graze in much the same way as geese, however they do also feed in water, 'up-ending' in true duck fashion from time to time.

Wigeon

NOVEMBER

YEAR 1	29th		30th
		Blackbird	
		Bluetit 3	
		Great tit 2	
		Collared dove	
Leeds, line dancing Tong			

YEAR 2	29th	CURRENT 9°C	30th
MAX 12.5°C MIN 3°C		MAX ~~13°C~~ 13°C MIN ~~3°C~~ 6.5°C	
		Collared dove 4	
		Bluetit 3	
		Greenfinch 24	
		Dunnock	
Grasmere		Return Grasmere	

YEAR 3	29th	Sunday wk 10.	30th
		Jay 2	
		Robin	
		Greenfinch 2	
Grasmere		Return from Grasmere	

ADDITIONAL NOTES:

2001. Very disappointing number of birds this month. 2 contributory factors. Much warmer than normal, lots of leaves on trees even at end of month. Increase in cats & a very aggressive squirrel feeding from table.

2002 Much better than last year despite still being warm & rather wet.

NOVEMBER

The tree sparrow, country cousin of the ubiquitous house sparrow, has been giving cause for concern. Recent surveys have revealed a dramatic decline in numbers. The population has fallen by 89 per cent over the last twenty-five years! Let us hope that this current trend can be halted, giving this charming little bird a chance to make a comeback.

Tree sparrow

DECEMBER CHECKLIST

YEAR — 1 2 3

DIVERS
- Red-throated diver
- Black-throated diver
- Great Northern diver

GREBES
- Little grebe
- Great crested grebe
- Red-necked grebe
- Slavonian grebe
- Black-necked grebe

SHEARWATERS
- Fulmar
- Cory's shearwater
- Great shearwater
- Sooty shearwater
- Manx shearwater
- Mediterranean shearwater

STORM PETRELS
- Storm petrel
- Leach's petrel

GANNETS
- Gannet

CORMORANTS
- Cormorant
- Shag

HERONS
- Bittern
- Night heron
- Little egret
- Great white egret
- Grey heron
- Purple heron

IBISES
- Spoonbill

DUCKS
- Mute swan
- Bewick's swan
- Whooper swan
- Bean goose
- Pink-footed goose
- White-fronted goose
- Greylag goose
- Snow goose
- Canada goose
- Barnacle goose
- Brent goose
- Egyptian goose
- Shelduck
- Mandarin
- Wigeon
- American wigeon
- Gadwall
- Teal
- Mallard
- Pintail
- Garganey
- Shoveler
- Red-crested pochard

YEAR — 1 2 3

DUCKS (cont.)
- Pochard
- Ring-necked duck
- Ferruginous duck
- Tufted duck
- Scaup
- Eider
- King eider
- Long-tailed duck
- Common scoter
- Surf scoter
- Velvet scoter
- Goldeneye
- Smew
- Red-breasted merganser
- Goosander
- Ruddy duck

HAWKS
- Honey buzzard
- Black kite
- Red kite
- White-tailed eagle
- Marsh harrier
- Hen harrier
- Montagu's harrier
- Goshawk
- Sparrowhawk
- Buzzard
- Rough-legged buzzard
- Golden eagle

OSPREYS
- Osprey

FALCONS
- Kestrel
- Red-footed falcon
- Merlin
- Hobby
- Peregrine

GROUSE
- Red grouse
- Ptarmigan
- Black grouse
- Capercaillie

PHEASANTS
- Red-legged partridge
- Grey partridge
- Quail
- Pheasant
- Golden pheasant
- Lady Amherst's pheasant

RAILS
- Water rail
- Spotted crake
- Corncrake
- Moorhen
- Coot

CRANES
- Crane

YEAR — 1 2 3

OYSTERCATCHERS
- Oystercatcher

AVOCETS
- Black-winged stilt
- Avocet

THICK-KNEES
- Stone curlew

PLOVERS
- Little ringed plover
- Ringed plover
- Kentish plover
- Dotterel
- Golden plover
- Grey plover
- Lapwing
- Turnstone

SANDPIPERS
- Knot
- Sanderling
- Little stint
- Temminck's stint
- White-rumped sandpiper
- Pectoral sandpiper
- Curlew sandpiper
- Purple sandpiper
- Dunlin
- Buff-breasted sandpiper
- Ruff
- Jack snipe
- Snipe
- Woodcock
- Black-tailed godwit
- Bar-tailed godwit
- Whimbrel
- Curlew
- Spotted redshank
- Redshank
- Marsh sandpiper
- Greenshank
- Green sandpiper
- Wood sandpiper
- Common sandpiper

PHALAROPES
- Red-necked phalarope
- Grey phalarope

SKUAS
- Pomarine skua
- Arctic skua
- Long-tailed skua
- Great skua

GULLS
- Mediterranean gull
- Little gull
- Sabine's gull
- Black-headed gull
- Ring-billed gull
- Common gull
- Lesser black-backed gull

YEAR — 1 2 3

GULLS (cont.)
- Herring gull
- Iceland gull
- Glaucous gull
- Great black-backed gull
- Kittiwake
- Sandwich tern
- Roseate tern
- Common tern
- Arctic tern
- Little tern
- Black tern
- White-winged black tern

AUKS
- Guillemot
- Razorbill
- Black guillemot
- Little auk
- Puffin

PIGEONS
- Rock dove
- Stock dove
- Wood-pigeon — ✓ ✓
- Collared dove — ✓ ✓
- Turtle dove

PARROTS
- Ring-necked parakeet

CUCKOOS
- Cuckoo

BARN OWLS
- Barn owl

OWLS
- Snowy owl
- Little owl
- Tawny owl
- Long-eared owl
- Short-eared owl

NIGHTJARS
- Nightjar

SWIFTS
- Swift
- Alpine swift

KINGFISHERS
- Kingfisher

BEE-EATERS
- Bee-eater

HOOPOES
- Hoopoe

WOODPECKERS
- Wryneck
- Green woodpecker
- Great spotted woodpecker.
- Lesser spotted woodpecker

LARKS
- Short-toed lark
- Woodlark
- Skylark
- Shore lark

YEAR — 1 2

SWALLOWS
- Sand martin
- Swallow
- House martin

PIPITS
- Richard's pipit
- Tawny pipit
- Tree pipit
- Meadow pipit
- Red-throated pipit
- Rock pipit
- Water pipit
- Yellow wagtail
- Grey wagtail
- Pied wagtail

WAXWINGS
- Waxwing

DIPPERS
- Dipper

WRENS
- Wren — ✓

ACCENTORS
- Dunnock — ✓ ✓

THRUSHES
- Robin — ✓ ✓
- Nightingale
- Bluethroat
- Black redstart
- Redstart
- Whinchat
- Stonechat
- Wheatear
- Ring ouzel
- Blackbird — ✓ ✓
- Fieldfare
- Song thrush
- Redwing
- Mistle thrush — ✓

FLYCATCHERS
- Cetti's warbler
- Grasshopper warbler
- Savi's warbler
- Aquatic warbler
- Sedge warbler
- Marsh warbler
- Reed warbler
- Icterine warbler
- Melodious warbler
- Dartford warbler
- Subalpine warbler
- Barred warbler
- Lesser whitethroat
- Whitethroat
- Garden warbler
- Blackcap
- Pallas's warbler
- Yellow-browed warbler
- Wood warbler

NON-LISTED SIGHTINGS

Teal are Britain's smallest ducks. They are 'dabblers', feeding on the surface of the water. Both sexes are attractive, but the drake with his chestnut head and green eyestripe, is particularly beautiful.

DECEMBER

YEAR 1	1st	Wk 10 Sunday. 2nd	3rd	TEMPS TAKEN 10pm each night 4th
				MAX MIN
Blackbird 2		Blackbird	Blackbird	Blackbird
Robin		Bluetit	Dunnock	Bluetit
Bluetit 2			Coal tit	Great tit 2
Great tit			Bluetit 2	
Dunnock			Great tit 2	
Sparrowhawks.				
Carrion Crow				
Collared dove				

YEAR 2 SUN. WK 10 CURRENT 10.5°C	1st	CURRENT 7°C 2nd	CURRENT 6.5°C 3rd	CURRENT 8.5°C 4th
MAX 12°C MIN 6.5°C		MAX 9°C MIN 5.5°C	MAX 8.5°C MIN 5.5°C	MAX 9°C MIN 2.5°C
Greenfinch 4 8&10 12		Starling	Blackbird 2	Greenfinch 8 9
Dunnock Starling.		Bluetit	Starling 2	Bluetit
Chaffinch (F) 2		Greenfinch 4 11	Greenfinch 2	Collared dove 2
Bluetit 2		Coal tit		Robin
Blackbird 2		Magpie		Magpie
Collared dove 34				Wren
Coal tit				
Robin				

YEAR 3	1st	2nd	3rd	4th
Greenfinch 2 5 & 11		Great tit	Crow	Collared dove 2
Chaffinch 2 3		Greenfinch 2	Greenfinch 39	Greenfinch
H. Sparrow 2		Magpie	Collared dove 2	Coal tit
Starling 9		Goldfinch 2	Coal tit	Blackbird
Bluetit		Chaffinch 2	Jay	Chaffinch
Coal tit 2		Collared dove 2	Chaffinch 2	Jay
Great tit		Coal tit	Blackbird	Magpie 3
Collared dove 2				
Jay 2		Grantham	P.A	

INSIDE   OUTSIDE

MAX ~~12°C~~ -13°C | MAX 17.5°C | | 7th
MIN 15°C - 0.5 5th | MIN 0.5°C | 6th |

INSIDE	OUTSIDE 6th	7th
Blackbird 23	Blackbird	
Shelit	Chaffinch	
	Robin	
	Bluetit 3	
	Greenfinch 2	
	Continent - Xmas Markets	

CURRENT 3°C 5th	CURRENT 6°C 6th	CURRENT 5.5°C 7th
MAX 7.5°C MIN 3°C	MAX 8.5°C MIN 4.5°C	MAX 10°C MIN 3.5°C
Bluetits 2	Blackbird	Collared dove 2
Magpie	Greenfinch x 4	Greenfinch x 10
Greenfinch 6	Bluetit	Starling
Robin	Dunnock	Bluetit
Dunnock	Coal tit 2	Chaffinch (M)
Wren	Robin	Blackbird 2
Collared dove 2	Crow	Dunnock 2
		Squirrel

5th	6th	SUN WR 11 7th
Chaffinch 2	Collared dove 2	Dunnock 2
Bluetit 2	Coal tit Jay	Robin
Greenfinch x 4	Chaffinch 23 Blackbird	Greenfinch 2
Jay 2	Magpie 2	Starling 2
Coal tit	Greenfinch 4	Bluetit 2
Robin	Bluetit	Chaffinch 2
Dunnock	Starling x 4	Collared dove 2
Blackbird	Great tit	Blackbird
Starling 3	Dunnock	

ADDITIONAL NOTES:

Blackcaps are members of the warbler family. It is only the male that has the black cap; the female's cap is brown. Most blackcaps are summer visitors to Britain; recently some birds have decided to overwinter, mostly in the south-west of the country.

Blackcap

DECEMBER

YEAR 1	8th	9th	10th	11th
		Sunday Wk 11	MAX 11°C MIN −0.5°C	? MAX 13.5°C MIN 4°C Bluetit
	Continent Xmas Mkts	Continent Xmas Markets	Continent Xmas Markets	

YEAR 2	8th	9th	10th	11th
	SUN WK 11. CURRENT 6°C MAX 8°C MIN 0°C	CURRENT 0.5°C MAX 7.5°C MIN 0°C	CURRENT 2°C MAX 7°C MIN −2.5°C	CURRENT −0.5°C MAX 10°C MIN −0.5°C
	Greenfinch ♂8 Starling ♂7	Collared dove 5	Chaffinch (M)	Collared dove 3
	Collared dove 2 Great tit 2	Greenfinch ♂5	Greenfinch ♂8	Blackbird 2
	Blackbird 23 Coal tit	Chaffinch	Blackbird 2	Greenfinch 3
	Dunnock	Blackbird 2	Coal tit 2	Starling
	Magpie (M F)	Dunnock	Starling ♂6	
	Chaffinch (F)(M F) 23	Robin	Dunnock	
	Wren	Starling ♂4	Collared dove 4	
	Bluetit 2	Bluetit		
	Robin			

YEAR 3	8th	9th	10th	11th
	Chaffinch 2 Goldfinch	Starling 6	Chaffinch 3	Jay
	Dunnock 2 Starling 4	Dunnock 2	Blackbird	Chaffinch
	Bluetit 2	Jay	Bluetit	Greenfinch ♂3
	Blackbird	Greenfinch 2	Goldfinch	Dunnock
	Jay	Chaffinch ♂4	Greenfinch 6	Starling 4
	Great tit 2	Blackbird	H.sparrow 3	H.sparrow
	Greenfinch	Great tit 2	Rook	Collared dove
	Magpie	Bluetit	Collared dove 3	Bluetit Squirrel
	Collared dove 23	(Heron flying in distance!)		

DECEMBER

ADDITIONAL NOTES:
9^ 2003 Heron flying in distance.

	12th
MAX 9.5°C	MIN 4.5°C
Magpie 2	
Bluetit 2	
Blackbird	
Collared dove	
Coal tit	

	13th
Max 9.5°C	MIN 1.5°C
3 greenfinches	
Collared dove	
Blackbird 2	
Chaffinch (F)	
Robin	
Coal tit	
Bluetit	

	14th
MAX 10.5°C	MIN 0°C
Bluetit 2	
Coal tit	
Blackbird	

		12th
CURRENT 1°C		
MAX	MIN	
Bluetit	Blackbird	
Robin		
Greenfinch 24		
Dunnock		
Wren		
Starling 5		
Collared dove 2		
Chaffinch (M)		

	13th
MAX 6.5°C	MIN 1.5°C
Bruges.	

	14th
CURRENT 4°C (10.30)	
MAX 7.5°C	MIN 3.5°C
Collared dove 2	
Greenfinch 58	
Chaffinch 2 (MF)	
Bluetit	
Blackbird 2	
Return Bruges	

	12th
Greenfinch 8	
Dunnock 2	
H. Sparrow 2	
Jay 2	
Chaffinch 3	
Blackbird	
Starling 2	
Collared dove	Squirrel

	13th
Greenfinch 8	
Dunnock 2	
Bluetit 2	
Chaffinch 2	
Jay	
Starling	
Blackbird	
Collared dove	

	14th
Sun 6°C 12	
Greenfinch 23	
Chaffinch 35	
Starling	
Collared dove 2	
Blackbird	
Jay	
Dunnock 2	
Bluetit	
Goldfinch 2	

The ptarmigan is only found on the mountain-tops of Scotland. Its plumage is its main form of protection from predators, with its coloration perfectly matching the bird's surroundings. In winter the birds turn white, becoming almost invisible in the snow.

Ptarmigan

DECEMBER

YEAR 1 15th	SUN. wk 12. 16th	17th	18th
MAX. 10.5°C MIN. 0°C	MAX 11°C MIN 0°C	MAX 11°C MIN 0°C	MAX 9.5°C MIN 0°C
Magpie	Starling	Bluetit	Collared dove 2
Collared dove	Coal tit	Coal tit	
Bluetit	Bluetit		
Coal tit	Chaffinch (F)		
Blackbird	Blackbird		
	Collared dove		

YEAR 2 Sun wk 12 CURRENT 4°C 15th	CURRENT 4°C 16th	CURRENT 2°C 17th	CURRENT -1°C 18th
MAX 5.5°C MIN 3.5°C	MAX 5°C MIN 1.5°C	MAX MIN	MAX 2.5°C MIN -3°C
Greenfinch 12	Chaffinch 2	Blackbird	Blackbird 3
Blackbird 3	Blackbird	Chaffinch 2	Starling 2
Bluetit	Coal tit	Greenfinch 5	Bluetit 2
Chaffinch	Bluetit		Dunnock
Starling 2	Greenfinch 5		Robin
Collared dove 2 & 5	Starling		Collared dove
Dunnock			Greenfinch
Squirrel			Frost

YEAR 3 15th	16th	17th	18th
Dunnock	Blackbird 2 Bluetit	Bluetit	Great tit
Greenfinch 2 3	Starling 4	Starling 4	Greenfinch 2
Chaffinch 2	Dunnock	Jay 2	Chaffinch 2 3 4
Blackbird 2	Greenfinch 2 4	Chaffinch 3 4	Jay
Collared dove 2	Chaffinch 2 3	Blackbird	Blackbird
Bluetit 2	Coal tit	Greenfinch	Starling 3
Starling	Jay 2	Dunnock	Bluetit 2
H. Sparrow	H Sparrow 2	Collared dove 2	Dunnock 2
	Collared dove 3	H. Sparrow	Goldfinch

DECEMBER

19th	20th	21st
MAX 8°C MIN 0.5°C	MAX 8°C MIN -0.5°C T.S MAX	SNOW SHOWER MIN -1°C
Collared dove 2	Collared dove	
Blackbird 2		
Robin		
Bluetit		
Magpie		

19th	20th	21st
CURRENT 0.5°C	CURRENT 3°C (12 o'clock)	CURRENT 2°C
MAX 5°C MIN 0.5°C	MAX 2.5°C MIN -2°C	MAX 7.5°C MIN 1.5°C
Blackbird 3	Starling 3	Blackbird 2 Dunnock
Greenfinch ♀3	Greenfinch 2	Bluetit 2
Bluetit 2	Blackbird	Greenfinch ♀4 5
Starling 2		Great tit ♂
Dunnock		Collared dove 2
Coal tit		Robin
Collared dove 2		Starling 5
Chaffinch (M)		Chaffinch 2 (MF)
Frost		

19th	Foggy & raining 20th	Sun. tot. 13. Fine, Strong 21st cold wind.
Blackbird 2 Bluetit	Blackbird 2 Goldfinch 3	Bluetit 2 Great tit
Starling 3 Goldfinch	Dunnock 2 H Sparrow 2	Greenfinch ♀♂ 10
Chaffinch ♀3	Chaffinch ♀3	Dunnock 2
Greenfinch 5	Greenfinch 25	Blackbird
Robin	Great tit	Chaffinch 23
Coal tit	Coal tit	Coal tit
H Sparrow	Starling	Collared dove ♀3
Collared dove	Jay Squirrel	Goldfinch
Magpie	Collared Dove 3	Starling

ADDITIONAL NOTES:

Hooded crows are found in Ireland and northern Scotland. Unlike their near relatives the carrion crows, they have grey bodies. In winter some 'Hoodies' can be seen further south in England.

Hooded crow

DECEMBER

YEAR 1 SNOW 22nd	23rd	24th	25th
MAX 2°C MIN -2°C	MAX 8°C MIN -2°C	MAX 10.5°C MIN 2°C	MAX 10.5°C MIN -2.5°
Blackbird	Thrush	Robin	
Coal tit	Blackbird	Blackbird	
Greenfinch	Bluetit 2	Collared dove 2	
Bluetit 2	Robin		
Collared dove	Greenfinch		
Chaffinch	Dunnock (F)		
Magpie 3	Coal tit		
Robin	Collared dove 3		
			Janet's

YEAR 2 SUN W23 CURRENT 6°C 22nd	CURRENT 9°C 23rd	CURRENT 10°C 24th	CURRENT 9.5°C (11.45am) 25th
MAX 10°C MIN 6°C	MAX 11.5°C MIN 7°C	MAX 13.5°C MIN 6°C	MAX 13°C MIN 5°C
Bluetit 2 Greenfinch 25	Bluetit 2	Greenfinch 12	Blackbird 4
Blackbird 4 Dunnock 2	Greenfinch 37	Magpie	Bluetit 2
Starling 6	Robin		Greenfinch 2
Great tit 2	Blackbird		Wren
Chaffinch (MF) 2	Chaffinch (MF) 2		
Robin	Starling 2		
Starling 4	Collared dove		
Wren			
Wood pigeon			JANET'S

YEAR 3 Cold + wet 22nd	Wet + grey, warm 23rd	Dull, warm 24th	Windy 25th
Great tit	Starlings	Collared dove 2 Robin	Blackbird
Chaffinch 3&5	Collared dove 4	Dunnock 2	
Greenfinch 35	Greenfinch 5	Chaffinch 2	
Blackbird	Chaffinch 3	Greenfinch 2 35	
Collared dove 2	Dunnock	Blackbird 2	
Dunnock 2	Blackbird 2	Starling 2	
Bluetit	Coal tit	Bluetit	
Starling 3	Jay	Great tit	
		Coal tit	Jackie's

DECEMBER

2002 28th 3 bullfinches family group from earlier in year menes 1 F?

9am. ↓ 26th	27th	28th
MAX 10·5°C MIN -2·5°C	MAX 8·5°C MIN 3°C	MAX 5·5°C MIN -0·5°C
Blackbird 23 (2m. F)		Blackbird 2
Collared dove		Bluetit
Bluetit 2		Magpie
Starling 2		Chaffinch
Greenfinch 23		Collared dove
RUGBY	RUGBY	(Gales)

26th	27th	28th
CURRENT 8°C MAX MIN	MAX 11·5°C MIN 5°C	CURRENT 6°C MAX 9·5°C MIN. 4°C
		Bullfinch 3 (MMF)
		Greenfinch 4
		Blackbird 2
		Great tit 2
		Bluetit 2
		Chaffinch
		Dunnock
RUGBY	RUGBY	Starling 2

26th	27th	Sun. cold. 28th
		Collared dove
		Greenfinch 2A6
		Starling
		Chaffinch 2
		Bluetit
		Blackbird
		Dunnock
		Goldfinch

Originally introduced in Roman times, the pheasant is widely distributed throughout Britain. The male birds are very attractive, bringing a welcome splash of colour to the winter landscape.

Pheasant

DECEMBER

YEAR 1 SNOW 29th	Vol 1. 1st Qtr 2002. Sun. 30th	31st
Max 1°C Min -1.5°C	MAX 3°C MIN -3.5°C	MAX 1°C MIN -3.5°C
Robin	Blackbird 3	Blackbird Chaffinch (F)
Chaffinch	Robin	Robin
Bluetit	Bluetit 2	Collared dove 2
Collared dove 2	Coal tit 2	Bluetit
Greenfinch	Woodpigeon	Great tit
Blackbird	Dunnock 2	Greenfinch
Magpie 2	Collared dove	Mistle Thrush
Dunnock 2	Great tit	Dunnock 2
Coal tit		

YEAR 2 SUN WK1 CURRENT 5.5° 29th	CURRENT 5°C 30th	CURRENT 3.5°C 31st
MAX 10.5°C MIN 4°C	MAX 7°C MIN 2°C	MAX 8°C MIN 2.5°C
Starling 3 Collared dove 3	Bluetit 2	Blackbird Crow
Bluetit Great tit	Chaffinch	Starling 3 Bullfinch (M)
Blackbird 2	Greenfinch 3&7	Bluetit 2 Wren
Greenfinch 2&8	Robin	Robin
Coal tit	Dunnock 2	Greenfinch 3&5&7
Chaffinch (M)(F)	Starling 4	Chaffinch 2
Bullfinch (M)(F)	Collared dove 3	Dunnock
Dunnock	Magpie	Collared dove 3

YEAR 3 Hard frost. 29th	Hard frost 30th	31st
Blackbird	Collared dove 2 Crow	Jay
Greenfinch 2	Blackbird 2	Blackbird
Goldfinch 2&3	Greenfinch 3	Dunnock 2
Dunnock 2	Dunnock	Bluetit 2
Starling 2	Great tit	Greenfinch 2
Bluetit 2	Jay	Chaffinch 2
Chaffinch	Chaffinch	Starling 2&3
Jay	Bluetit 2	Collared dove 2
	Starling 2	Great tit

ADDITIONAL NOTES:

A few pairs of snow buntings breed in the Scottish mountains, but most birds are winter visitors to Britain. At this time of the year, they can sometimes be seen feeding in flocks around the coast.

Snow bunting